THE ANCIENT FAITH PSALTER

✠ ✠ ✠

TRANSLATED BY
*Monks of the
Orthodox Church*

ANCIENT FAITH PUBLISHING
CHESTERTON, INDIANA

The Ancient Faith Psalter
Translation © 2016 Ancient Faith Publishing

Published by:
Ancient Faith Publishing
A Division of Ancient Faith Ministries
1050 Broadway, Ste 14
Chesterton, IN 46304

Large print edition ISBN: 978-1-955890-46-5

Printed in the United States of America

CONTENTS

INTRODUCTION

THE PSALTER is the prayer book of the Church. It has been so since before there was a Christian Church. There is an ancient saying, attributed to St. Athanasius the Great, that "the Psalms are different from the rest of Scripture in that while the rest of Scripture speaks to us, the Psalms speak for us." When we pray the Psalms, we are praying the words God has given us to pray. It has also been said that the story of God's dealings with Israel is an allegory of each person's spiritual journey, the story of God's dealings with every human soul. Therefore, inasmuch as the Psalms sum up and interpret the story of Israel, the Psalms also sum up and interpret the spiritual journey of every human being.

The Psalms touch every experience of human life in our fallen world. Every joy and every terror, every fear and every hope are found expressed in the Psalms. Some psalms are beautiful, to the point of seeming sentimental; others are bloody and apparently vindictive. Such a range of emotion and experience is offered to us in prayer because in some inner or outer way, at some time in our life, we will all experience this full range of thoughts and feelings. In fact, because some of these thoughts and feelings are so extreme, so evidently horrible, it is only through praying the Psalms that we come to realize and then confess to ourselves and to God in prayer that yes, even such terrible things as these have at one time or another passed through our minds and perhaps even our hands.

This literal reading of the Psalms, however, is only the beginning. As one prays the Psalms, one soon begins to realize that the enemy, the Amalekite or Philistine, the nations that rage against God, are not people or situations outside myself but are most poignantly referring to the wicked impulses and evil thoughts I must battle within myself. The Psalmist's cry for deliverance becomes my own as I see within my own heart and mind the struggle between good and evil, the betraying thought, the accusing word, or the mocking laugh. The Psalms give us words, images, and metaphors by which we can cry out to God for help in the midst of our inner struggles. What the Psalmist describes as external speaks to our inner struggles because all outer conflict is a reflection of inner struggle. Is this not what Jesus told us—it is out of the heart that murders and adultery flow (Matt. 15:19)?

The Psalter is a prophetic book. It speaks prophetically of Christ, but it also speaks prophetically of all who are in Christ. Just as "strong bulls surround" Christ on the Cross, so too all who pick up their cross and follow Christ experience, in one form or another, this attack of the strong and come to know their own weakness in resisting it, their own need to be delivered from "the power of the dog . . . the mouth of the lion . . . [and] the horns of the wild bulls." Similarly, the prophetic declaration of the Resurrection of Christ, "Let God arise, let His enemies be scattered," is also our declaration as we experience moments of deliverance and help over our inner enemies. The Psalms speak of God and man, Christ and Christian, inner and outer conflict, victory and defeat, heaven and earth, wisdom and foolishness. With few words and much meaning, the Psalms provide the images and words for every prayer, every need, every celebration on our journey through this world.

ABOUT THIS EDITION

The Psalter is the most quoted biblical book in the liturgical prayers of the Orthodox Church. This edition of the Psalter is intended for prayer (either at home or in church) rather than for reference.* In keeping with this purpose, the Psalms are not presented in regular numerical order. Psalms 120 through 134 follow Psalm 150, and then Psalms 110 through 119 follow Psalm 134. This is because this Psalter is organized according to the cycle of daily readings according to the monastic practice in the Orthodox Church.

The Psalter is divided into twenty sections

---

*For reference purposes, we recommend the Book of Psalms found in *The Orthodox Study Bible*.

called *kathismata*. Each *kathisma* is then divided into three smaller sections called *stases*. In typical monastic practice, two kathismata are read every morning as part of Matins, and one kathisma is read each evening as part of Vespers. In this way the entire Psalter is prayed each week.

However, if you are just beginning to pray the Psalter, we recommended that you start by praying out loud (perhaps with a slight chant intonation) only one stasis a day. Regularity is much more important than volume in praying the Psalter. As you pray through the Psalter year after year, you will discover that the words of the Psalms become an ongoing conversation between you and your God.

A word about the text. The text is based on an English translation of the Masoretic Hebrew text corrected to the Septuagint and other ancient witnesses (Dead Sea Scrolls, etc.). Consequently, the numbering of the Psalms is according to the Hebrew, which we consider easier for most English readers to use. (The Septuagint numbering is included in parentheses for those who prefer it.) The text was also corrected to conform to the liturgical use of the Orthodox Church. Finally, the text was corrected for readability. The goal is a text that is faithful, majestic, and easy to understand when read or chanted aloud.

PSALM 1

Blessed is the man who walks not in the
counsel of the wicked, nor stands on the
path of sinners, nor sits in the seat of
scoffers;

but his delight is in the law of the Lord, and
on His law he meditates day and night.

He is like a tree planted by streams of water,
that yields its fruit in its season, and its
leaf does not wither.

In all that he does, he prospers.

The wicked are not so, but are like chaff
which the wind drives away.

Therefore the wicked will not stand in the
judgment, nor sinners in the congregation
of the righteous;

for the Lord knows the way of the
righteous, but the way of the wicked will
perish.

Why do the nations conspire, and the peoples plot in vain?

The kings of the earth set themselves, and the rulers of the people have assembled, against the Lord and His Anointed, saying,

"Let us burst their bonds asunder and cast their cords from us."

He who sits in the heavens laughs; the Lord has them in derision.

Then He will speak to them in His wrath and terrify them in His fury.

But I have been made King by Him on Zion, His holy hill, telling the decree of the Lord:

"The Lord said to Me, 'You are My Son, this day have I begotten You.'"

Ask of me, and I will give You the nations for Your inheritance, and the ends of the earth as Your dominion.

You shall break them with a rod of iron and dash them in pieces like a potter's vessel.

Now therefore, O kings, be wise; be warned, O rulers of the earth.

Serve the Lord with fear, and rejoice in
  Him with trembling.
Accept correction, lest He be angry and you
  perish from the righteous way; for His
  wrath is quickly kindled.
Blessed are all who take refuge in Him.

PSALM 3

O Lord, how many are my foes! Many are
  rising against me; many are saying of me,
  "There is no help for him in God."
But You, O Lord, are a shield about me, my
  glory and the lifter of my head.
I cry aloud to the Lord, and He answers me
  from His holy hill.
I lie down and sleep; I wake again, for the
  Lord sustains me.
I am not afraid of ten thousands of people
  who have set themselves against me round
  about.
Arise, O Lord! Deliver me, O my God!
For You strike all my enemies on the cheek;
  You break the teeth of the wicked.
Deliverance belongs to the Lord; Your
  blessing be upon Your people!

KATHISMA 1—STASIS II

PSALM 4

The Lord hears me when I call to Him!

You have given me room when I was in distress; have compassion on me and hear my prayer.

O sons of men, how long will you be slow of heart? How long will you love vain words and seek after lies?

But know that the Lord has done wonderful things for His Holy One: the Lord hears when I call to Him.

Be angry, but sin not; feel compunction on your beds for what you say in your hearts.

Offer a sacrifice of righteousness and put your trust in the Lord.

There are many who say, "Oh, that we might see some good!"

The light of Your countenance has left its imprint on us, O Lord!

You have put more joy in my heart than
they have when their grain and wine
abound.

In peace and confidence I will both lie
down and sleep; for You alone, O Lord,
cause me to dwell in hope.

PSALM 5

Give ear to my words, O Lord; give heed to
my groaning.

Hearken to the sound of my cry, my King
and my God, for to You do I pray.

O Lord, in the morning You hear my voice;
in the morning I prepare a sacrifice for
You and watch.

For You are not a God who delights
in wickedness; evil may not sojourn
with You.

The boastful may not stand before Your
eyes; You hate all evildoers.

You destroy those who speak lies; the Lord
abhors bloodthirsty and deceitful men.

But I, through the abundance of Your
mercy, will enter Your house; I will

worship toward Your holy temple in the fear of You.

Lead me, O Lord, in Your righteousness because of my enemies; make Your way straight before me.

For there is no truth in their mouth; their heart is destruction, their throat is an open sepulcher, they flatter with their tongue.

Make them bear their guilt, O God; let them fall by their own counsels;

because of their many transgressions cast them out, for they have rebelled against You.

But let all who take refuge in You rejoice, let them ever sing for joy;

and defend them, that those who love Your name may exult in You.

For You bless the righteous, O Lord; You cover him with favor as with a shield.

PSALM 6

O Lord, rebuke me not in Your anger nor chasten me in Your wrath.

Have mercy on me, O Lord, for I am weak;
heal me, for my bones are troubled.

My soul also is sorely troubled. But You,
O Lord—how long?

Turn, O Lord, save my life; deliver me for
the sake of Your mercy.

For in death there is no remembrance of
You; in Sheol who can give You praise?

I am weary with my moaning; every night
I flood my bed with tears; I drench my
couch with my weeping.

My eye wastes away because of grief; it
grows weak because of all my foes.

Depart from me, all you workers of evil;
for the Lord has heard the sound of my
weeping.

The Lord has heard my supplication; the
Lord accepts my prayer.

All my enemies shall be ashamed and sorely
troubled; they shall turn back and be put
to shame in a moment.

☩ ☩ ☩

PSALM 7

O Lord my God, I have set my hope on
   You; save me from all my pursuers and
   deliver me,

lest like a lion they rend me, dragging me
   away with none to rescue.

O Lord my God, if I have done this, if there
   is wrong in my hands, if I dealt back evil
   to those dealing evil to me,

then may I fall empty because of my enemy;
   let the enemy pursue me and overtake me,

and let him trample my life to the ground
   and lay my soul in the dust.

Arise, O Lord, in Your anger; lift Yourself
   up against the fury of my enemies;

Arise, O Lord my God, in the decree which
   You have commanded,

and the assembly of peoples will surround
   You. Over it take Your seat on high.

The Lord shall judge the people. Give
   me justice, O Lord, according to my
   righteousness and according to the
   integrity that is in me.

Oh, let the evil of the wicked come to an
end, but establish the righteous,
You who sound the depths of hearts and
reins, O righteous God.
My righteous help is from God, who saves
the upright in heart.
God is a righteous judge, strong and patient,
who does not make His wrath felt
every day.
If you will not repent, God will whet His
sword; He has bent His bow and made it
ready.
On it He has fitted instruments of death;
He has fashioned His arrows for those
who rage.
Behold, the wicked man conceives evil, and
is pregnant with mischief, and brings
forth lies.
He makes a pit, digging it out, and falls into
the hole which he has made.
His mischief returns upon his own
head, and on his own pate his violence
descends.

I will give to the Lord the thanks due to His righteousness, and I will sing praise to the name of the Lord, the Most High.

PSALM 8

O Lord, our Lord, how majestic is Your name in all the earth, for Your glory is chanted above the heavens;

out of the mouths of babes and infants, You have fashioned perfect praise in response to Your foes, to still the enemy and the avenger.

When I look at Your heavens, the work of Your fingers, the moon and the stars which You have established;

what is man that You are mindful of him, or the son of man that You take care of him?

You have made him a little lower than the angels; You have crowned him with glory and honor;

You have given him dominion over the works of Your hands; You have put all things under his feet,

all sheep and oxen, and also the beasts of the field, the birds of the air, and the fish of

the sea, whatever passes along the paths of
the sea.

O Lord, our Lord, how majestic is Your
name in all the earth!

✠ ✠ ✠

KATHISMA 2—STASIS I

PSALM 9 (9A)

I will give thanks to You, O Lord, with
my whole heart; I will proclaim all Your
wonders.

I will be glad and exult in You; I will sing
praise to Your name, O Most High.

When my enemies are turned back, they
will stumble and perish before Your Face.

For You have maintained my just cause; You
have sat on the throne giving righteous
judgment.

You have rebuked the nations, and the
ungodly one has perished; You have
blotted out their name forever and ever.

The swords of the enemy have utterly
failed; their cities You have destroyed;
the very memory of them has perished in
tumult.

But the Lord reigns forever; He has
established His throne for judgment,

and He judges the world with righteousness;
He judges the peoples with equity.

The Lord is a stronghold for the oppressed,
   a stronghold in times of trouble.
And those who know Your name put their
   trust in You, for You, O Lord, have not
   forsaken those who attentively seek You.
Sing praises to the Lord, who dwells in
   Zion! Tell among the peoples His deeds!
For He who avenges blood is mindful of
   them; He does not forget the cry of the
   afflicted.
Have mercy on me, O Lord! Look on the
   affliction I suffer from those who hate me.
You lift me up from the gates of death, that
   I may recount all Your praises,
that in the gates of the daughter of Zion I
   may rejoice in Your deliverance.
The nations have sunk in the pit which they
   made; in the net which they hid has their
   own foot been caught.
The Lord has made Himself known; He has
   executed judgment; the wicked are snared
   in the work of their own hands.
Let sinners be driven to Sheol, all the
   nations that forget God.

For the needy shall not always be forgotten,
and the hope of the poor shall not perish
forever.

Arise, O Lord! Let not man prevail; let the
nations be judged before You!

Appoint a lawgiver over them; let the
nations know that they are but men!

PSALM 10 (9B)

Why do You stand far off, O Lord? Why
do You overlook us in times of trouble?

In arrogance the ungodly hotly pursue
the poor;

let them be caught in the schemes which
they have devised.

For the sinner boasts of the desires of his
heart, and the unjust one blesses himself.

The sinner has provoked the Lord; in his
pride he does not seek Him; God is not
before him.

His ways are profane at all times; Your
judgments are removed from him; as for
all his foes, he gains mastery over them.

For he says in his heart, "I shall not be moved; throughout all generations I shall not meet adversity."

His mouth is filled with cursing and deceit and oppression; under his tongue are mischief and iniquity.

He sits in ambush with the rich in order to murder the innocent.

His eyes stealthily watch for the poor; he lurks in secret like a lion in his covert;

he lurks that he may seize the poor; he seizes the poor when he draws him into his net.

Yet he himself will fall when he has overcome the poor.

For he has said in his heart, "God has forgotten; He has hidden His Face; He will never see it."

Arise, O Lord my God, and let Your hand be lifted up; do not forget Your poor forever.

Why does the wicked renounce God and say in his heart, "You will not call to account!"

But You do see, for You perceive suffering
and pain, that You may take them into
Your hands;

the poor man commits himself to You; You
have been the helper of the fatherless.

Break the arm of the sinner and evildoer;
may his sin be sought for and not be
found.

The Lord is king forever and ever; the
nations shall perish from His land.

O Lord, You will hear the desire of the
poor; You will strengthen their heart;

You will incline Your ear to do justice to the
fatherless and the oppressed, so that men
may not boast any more upon the earth.

PSALM 11 (10)

In the Lord I take refuge; how can you
say to me, "Flee like a bird to the
mountains"?

For lo, the wicked bend the bow, they have
prepared their arrows for the quiver, to
shoot in secret at the upright in heart.

They have pulled down what You have
built, and what has the Righteous done?

The Lord is in His holy temple; the Lord's throne is in heaven; His eyes behold the poor; His eyelids test the sons of men.

The Lord tests the righteous and the wicked; one that loves violence hates his own soul.

On the wicked He will rain coals of fire and brimstone; a scorching wind shall be the portion of their cup.

For the Lord is righteous; He loves righteous deeds; His Face looks upon honor.

✠ ✠ ✠

KATHISMA 2—STASIS II

PSALM 12 (11)

Save me, O Lord; for there is no longer any that is godly; for truth has vanished from among the sons of men.

Everyone utters lies to his neighbor; with flattering lips and a double heart they speak.

May the Lord cut off all flattering lips, the tongue that makes great boasts, those who say, "With our tongue we will prevail; our lips are with us; who is our master?"

"Because of the suffering of the poor, because the needy groan, I will now arise," says the Lord;

"I will set myself for salvation and not draw back from it!"

The Lord's words are pure words, like silver refined in a furnace on the ground, purified seven times.

You, O Lord, shall protect us and preserve us from this generation forever.

On every side the wicked prowl, yet according to Your greatness You have greatly exalted the sons of men.

PSALM 13 (12)

How long, O Lord? Will You forget me until the end? How long will You turn away Your Face from me?

How long shall I take counsel in my soul and have sorrows in my heart every day? How long shall my enemy be exalted over me?

Consider and answer me, O Lord my God;
   lighten my eyes, lest I sleep in death;
lest at any time my enemies say, "I
   have prevailed against him"; lest my
   persecutors exult if ever I am shaken.
But I have trusted in Your mercy; my heart
   shall rejoice in Your salvation.
I will sing to the Lord, because He has
   dealt bountifully with me, and I will
   sing psalms to the name of the Lord
   Most High.

PSALM 14 (13)

The fool says in his heart, "There is
   no God."
They are corrupt; they do abominable
   deeds; there is none that does good.
The Lord looked down from heaven and
   saw all the sons of men, to see if there
   are any that have understood, that sought
   after God.
They have all fallen away; they are all alike
   unprofitable; there is none that does good,
   no, not one.

Shall they never learn, those who practice
lawlessness, those who eat up my people
as they eat bread? They do not call
upon God.

There they were in great terror, where there
was no cause for fear, for God dwells
among the righteous.

They tried to confound the plans of the
poor, but the Lord is his hope.

Who will bring about the salvation of Israel
out of Zion?

When the Lord brings back the captives of
His people, Jacob will rejoice and Israel
be glad.

✠ ✠ ✠

KATHISMA 2—STASIS III

PSALM 15 (14)

O Lord, who shall sojourn in Your
tabernacle? Who shall dwell on Your holy
mountain?

He who walks blamelessly, and does what is
right, and speaks truth from his heart;

who has not spoken deceitfully with his
tongue, and does no evil to his neighbor,
nor takes up a reproach against his
brother;
in whose eyes the Evil One is despised, but
who glorifies those who fear the Lord;
who swears an oath to his neighbor and
does not break it;
who does not put out his money at interest,
and does not take a bribe against the
innocent.
He who does these things shall never be
moved.

PSALM 16 (15)

Preserve me, O God, for in You do I take
refuge.
I say to the Lord, "You are my Lord, for You
have no need of my goodness."
As for the saints in the land, the Lord has
made them wonderful; all His will is
accomplished in them.
The weaknesses of those who choose
another god have been multiplied: "I will

not attend their meetings of blood or take
their names upon my lips."

The Lord is the portion of my inheritance
and of my cup; You restore to me my
inheritance.

The lines have fallen for me in the best of
places; yes, I have an excellent heritage.

I will bless the Lord who gives me counsel;
even in the night my heart instructs me.

I keep the Lord always before me; because
He is at my right hand, I shall not be
shaken.

Therefore my heart is glad, and my soul
rejoices; my body also dwells securely.

For You will not leave my soul in Sheol nor
let Your Holy One see corruption.

You have shown me the paths of life;
You will fill me with the joy of Your
countenance; at Your right hand are
pleasures forevermore.

PSALM 17 (16)

Hear a just cause, O Lord; attend to my
cry! Give ear to my prayer from lips free
of deceit!

From You let my vindication come! Let my
eyes see the right!

If You try my heart, if You visit me by
night, if You test me,

You will find no wickedness in me; my
mouth does not transgress.

With regard to the works of men, by the
word of Your lips I have avoided the ways
of the violent.

My steps have held fast to Your paths; my
feet have not slipped.

I call upon You, for You will answer me,
O God; incline Your ear to me, hear
my words.

Wondrously show Your steadfast love,
O Savior of those who seek refuge from
their adversaries at Your right hand.

Keep me as the apple of the eye; hide me
in the shadow of Your wings from the
wicked who despoil me, my deadly
enemies who surround me.

They close their hearts to pity; with their
mouths they speak arrogantly.

They track me down; now they surround
me; they set their eyes to cast me to the
ground.

They are like a lion eager to tear, as a young
lion lurking in ambush.

Arise, O Lord! Confront them, overthrow
them!

Deliver my life from the wicked by Your
sword, from men by Your hand, O Lord,
from men whose portion in life is of the
world.

May their belly be filled with what You
have stored up for them;

may their children have more than enough;
may they leave something over to their
babes.

As for me, I shall behold Your Face in
righteousness;

when I awake, I shall be satisfied with
beholding Your form.

✠ ✠ ✠

KATHISMA 3—STASIS I

PSALM 18 (17)

I will love You, O Lord, my God. The Lord is my refuge, my strength and my deliverer.

My God is my helper; in Him will I hope: my shield and the horn of my salvation, my defender.

I call upon the Lord with songs of praise, and I shall be saved from my enemies.

The waves of death engulfed me; the torrents of perdition assailed me;

The pangs of Sheol surrounded me; the snares of death overtook me.

In my distress I called upon the Lord; to my God I cried for help.

From His temple He heard my voice, and my cry to Him reached His ears.

Then the earth reeled and rocked; the foundations also of the mountains were troubled and shaken, because He was angry with them.

Smoke went up from His anger and
   devouring fire from His mouth that
   kindled coals into flame.

He bowed the heavens and came down;
   thick darkness was under His feet.

He rode upon cherubim and flew, borne
   upon the wings of the wind.

He made darkness His hiding place; as His
   canopy around Him, dark thunderclouds
   hung in the sky.

Out of the brightness before Him there
   broke through the clouds hailstones and
   coals of fire.

Then the Lord thundered from heaven, and
   the Most High uttered His voice.

He shot His arrows and scattered them; with
   many lightning flashes He routed them.

Then the fountains of waters appeared,
   and the foundations of the earth were
   laid bare

at Your rebuke, O Lord, at the blast of the
   breath of Your anger.

He reached from on high and took me; He
   drew me out of the deep waters.

He delivered me from my strong enemies
and from those who hated me, for they
were mightier than I.

They overtook me in the day of my
calamity, but the Lord was my firm
support.

He brought me forth into a spacious place;
He will deliver me, because He delights
in me.

The Lord will reward me according to my
righteousness; according to the cleanness
of my hands He will repay me.

For I have kept the ways of the Lord and
have not acted wickedly toward my God.

For all His judgments are before me, and
His statutes have not departed from me.

I shall be blameless toward Him, and I will
keep myself from iniquity.

The Lord will reward me according to my
righteousness, according to the cleanness
of my hands in His sight.

With the holy You will be holy; with the
innocent You will be innocent.

With the great You will be great, and with
the perverse You will be perverse.

For You will save a humble people, and you
will humble the eyes of the proud.

For You will light my lamp, O Lord my
God; You will enlighten my darkness.

For with Your help, I shall be delivered
from a troop, and in my God I shall leap
over the wall.

As for my God, His way is perfect; the
words of the Lord are tried by fire; He is
the defender of all who hope in Him.

For who is God but the Lord? And who is
God but our God?

It is God who girded me with strength and
made my way blameless.

He made my feet like hinds' feet and set me
secure on the heights.

He trained my hands for war so that my
arms can bend a bow of bronze.

You have given me the shield of salvation,
and Your right hand has supported me.

Your instruction set me on the straight path
forever; Your instruction itself taught me.

You gave length to my steps under me, and
unwavering was my stride.

I will pursue my enemies and catch them,
and I will not turn back till they are
destroyed.
I will crush them, and they will not be able
to stand; they will fall under my feet.
For You girded me with strength for war;
You bound the feet of all my adversaries
beneath me.
You made my enemies turn their backs to
me, and those who hated me You have
utterly destroyed.
They cried out, but there was none to save;
they cried to the Lord, but He did not
answer them.
I will beat them fine as dust before the
wind; I cast them out like the mire of the
streets.
You deliver me from strife with the peoples;
You make me the head of the nations.
A people whom I had not known became
my servants; as soon as they heard me,
they obeyed me.
But my sons became strangers to me; they
lied to me; my sons, having estranged

themselves, grew old, and limping, they
strayed from their path.

The Lord lives; blessed be my God! Exalted
be the God of my salvation!

God gives vengeance to me and subdues
peoples under me.

You who deliver me from my angry enemies
will exalt me above those who rise
against me; You will deliver me from the
unrighteous man.

For this I will extol You, O Lord, among the
nations and sing praise to Your name.

God works wonders for the salvation of His
King and deals mercifully with David His
Anointed and his seed forever.

☩ ☩ ☩

KATHISMA 3—STASIS II

PSALM 19 (18)

The heavens are telling the glory of
God; and the firmament proclaims His
handiwork.

Day to day pours forth speech, and night to night declares knowledge.

There are no tongues or words in which their voices are not heard.

Their proclamation has gone out into all the earth and their words to the ends of the universe.

He has set His tabernacle in the sun; like a bridegroom coming forth from his bridal chamber, like a strong man it runs its course with joy.

Its rising is from one end of the heavens and its circuit to the other end; no one can escape from its heat.

The law of the Lord is perfect, converting souls; the testimony of the Lord is sure, making children wise.

The precepts of the Lord are right, rejoicing the heart; the commandment of the Lord is bright, enlightening the eyes.

The fear of the Lord is pure, enduring forever and ever; the judgments of the Lord are true and righteous altogether.

More to be desired are they than gold or
  precious stones and sweeter than honey or
  the honeycomb.
So Your servant keeps them; in keeping
  them there is great reward.
Who can discern his transgressions?
Cleanse me from my hidden faults, and
  preserve Your servant from those which
  are foreign to me.
If they do not have dominion over me, I
  shall be blameless and innocent of great
  transgression.
Then the words of my mouth will be
  pleasing to You;
and the meditation of my heart will be
  before You always, O Lord, my helper and
  my Redeemer.

PSALM 20 (19)

The Lord answer you in the day of trouble;
  the name of the God of Jacob protect you!
May He send you help from the sanctuary
  and give you support from Zion!

May He remember all your sacrifices and
regard with favor your whole burnt
offerings!

May He grant you your heart's desire and
fulfill all your plans!

We will rejoice in your salvation and be
exalted in the name of the Lord our God.
May the Lord fulfill all your petitions!

Now I know that the Lord has saved His
Anointed; He will answer him from His
holy heaven; salvation is in the mighty
deeds of His right hand.

Some trust in chariots and some in horses;
but we will call upon the name of the
Lord our God.

Their feet have been fettered; they have
fallen, but we have risen and stand
upright.

Save the king, O Lord; hear us on the day
we call.

PSALM 21 (20)

In Your strength the king rejoices, O Lord,
and greatly exults in Your salvation!

You have given him his heart's desire and
  have not withheld the request of his lips.
For You meet him with goodly blessings;
  You have placed upon his head a crown of
  precious stones.
He asked life of You, and You gave it to
  him—length of days forever and ever.
His glory is great in Your salvation; splendor
  and majesty You have bestowed upon him.
You will give him a blessing forever and
  will make him glad with the joy of Your
  presence.
For the king hopes in the Lord; and
  through the mercy of the Most High he
  shall not be shaken.
May your hand be felt by all your enemies;
  may your right hand find all those who
  hate you.
You will make them like a blazing oven on
  the day when you appear; the Lord will
  confound them in His wrath; and fire will
  consume them.
You will destroy their fruit from the earth
  and their seed from among the sons
  of men.

For they planned evil against you; they have
    devised plots which will not succeed.

For you will put them to flight; you will
    make them face your remnant.

Be exalted, O Lord, in Your strength! We
    will sing and praise Your power!

✠ ✠ ✠

KATHISMA 3—STASIS III

PSALM 22 (21)

O God, my God, attend to me! Why have
    You forsaken me?

Why are You so far from helping me, from
    the words of my groaning?

O my God, I cry by day, but You do not
    answer, and by night, but find no rest.

But You dwell in the sanctuary, the Praise of
    Israel.

In You our fathers hoped; they hoped in
    You, and You delivered them.

To You they cried and were saved; in You
    they hoped and were not disappointed.

But as for me, I am a worm and no man, a reproach of men and the outcast of the people.

All who see me mock me; they open their lips and wag their heads:

"He hoped in the Lord—let Him deliver him; let Him save him, if He was pleased in Him."

Yet You are He who took me from the womb; You have been my hope from my mother's breasts.

Upon You was I cast from my birth; from my mother's womb, You have been my God.

Be not far from me, for trouble is near, and there is none to help me.

Many bullocks encircle me; strong bulls surround me.

They open their mouths against me like ravenous and roaring lions.

I am poured out like water, and all my bones are out of joint; my heart is like wax melted within my breast.

My strength is dried up like a potsherd, and
my tongue cleaves to my throat; You have
brought me down into the dust of death.

For many dogs are round about me; a
company of evildoers closes in upon me;
they have pierced my hands and feet.

They count all my bones; they stare and
gloat over me.

They divided my garments among them,
and for my raiment they cast lots.

But You, O Lord, do not remove Your help
from me! Hasten to my aid!

Deliver me from the sword, my afflicted
soul from the power of the dog!

Save me from the mouth of the lion,
my lowliness from the horns of the
wild bulls.

I will declare Your name to my brethren;
in the midst of the assembly I will
confess You.

Praise Him, all who fear the Lord! All you
sons of Jacob, glorify Him, and stand in
awe of Him, all you offspring of Israel!

For He has not despised or abhorred the
supplication of the poor man, nor has

He turned His Face from me, but He has heard me when I cried to Him.

From You is my praise; in the great congregation I will praise You; I will pay my vows in the presence of those who fear You.

The poor shall eat and be satisfied; those who seek the Lord shall praise Him; their hearts shall live forever.

All the ends of the earth shall remember and turn to the Lord; all the families of the nations shall bow down before Him.

For the Kingdom belongs to the Lord, and He Himself rules over the nations.

All the mighty ones of the earth have bowed down; before Him shall bow all who go down into the earth.

Yes, my soul lives for Him, and my children will serve Him.

The coming generation shall be told of the Lord, and they will declare His righteousness to a people yet unborn whom the Lord has made.

PSALM 23 (22)

The Lord is my shepherd; I shall not want;
   He makes me lie down in green pastures;
He establishes me beside the waters of rest;
   He restores my soul.
He leads me in the paths of righteousness
   for His name's sake.
Even though I walk through the valley of
   the shadow of death, I will fear no evil;
   for You are with me;
Your rod and Your staff, they comfort me.
You prepare a table before me in the
   presence of my enemies;
You anoint my head with oil: oh, how
   exquisite is the inebriation of Your cup!
Your mercy, O Lord, shall follow me all the
   days of my life, and I shall dwell in the
   house of the Lord forever.

PSALM 24 (23)

The earth is the Lord's and its fullness, the
   world and all that dwell in it.
He has founded it upon the seas and
   established it upon the rivers.

Who shall ascend the mountain of the
   Lord, and who shall stand in His holy
   place?
He that is innocent in his hands and pure in
   his heart, who has not lifted up his soul
   to vanity nor sworn deceitfully to his
   neighbor.
He will receive a blessing from the Lord
   and mercy from God his Savior.
This is the generation of those who seek
   Him, who seek the Face of the God of
   Jacob.
Lift up your gates, O you princes, and be
   lifted up, O everlasting doors, and the
   King of glory shall enter.
Who is this King of glory? The Lord,
   strong and mighty, the Lord, mighty in
   battle.
Lift up your gates, O you princes, and be
   lifted up, O everlasting doors, and the
   King of glory shall enter.
Who is this King of glory? The Lord of
   hosts, He is the King of glory!

KATHISMA 4—STASIS I

PSALM 25 (24)

To You, O Lord, I lift up my soul. O my
   God, in You I trust;

let me not be put to shame; let not my
   enemies exult over me.

Yes, let none that wait for You be put to
   shame; let them be ashamed who are
   wantonly treacherous.

Make me to know Your ways, O Lord; teach
   me Your paths.

Lead me in Your truth and teach me, for
   You are the God of my salvation; for You I
   wait all the day long.

Be mindful of Your mercy, O Lord, and of
   Your steadfast love, for they have been
   from of old.

Remember not the sins of my youth or my
   transgressions;

according to Your steadfast love, remember
   me for Your goodness' sake, O Lord!

Good and upright is the Lord; therefore He instructs sinners in the way.

He leads the humble in what is right and teaches the humble His way.

All the paths of the Lord are steadfast love and faithfulness for those who keep His covenant and His testimonies.

For Your name's sake, O Lord, pardon my guilt, for it is great.

Who is the man that fears the Lord?

Him will He instruct in the way that he should choose.

His soul shall dwell with the blessed and his children shall possess the land.

The friendship of the Lord is for those who fear Him, and He makes known to them His covenant.

My eyes are ever toward the Lord, for He will pluck my feet out of the net.

Turn to me and be gracious to me, for I am lonely and afflicted.

Relieve the troubles of my heart and bring me out of my distresses.

Consider my affliction and my trouble and forgive all my sins.

Consider how many are my foes and with
what violent hatred they hate me.

Oh, guard my life and deliver me; let me not
be put to shame, for I take refuge in You.

May integrity and uprightness preserve me,
for I wait for You.

Redeem Israel, O God, out of all his
troubles!

PSALM 26 (25)

Judge me, O Lord, for I have walked in my
innocence; I have hoped in the Lord and
shall not be moved.

Prove me, O Lord, and try me; test with fire
my reins and my heart.

For Your mercy is before my eyes, and I
rejoice in Your truth.

I have not sat with a vain council, nor do I
consort with transgressors;

I have hated the company of evildoers, and I
will not sit with the ungodly.

I will wash my hands in innocence, and go
about Your altar, O Lord,

proclaiming Your name, telling of all Your
wonders.

O Lord, I love the beauty of Your house and
the place where Your glory dwells.

Do not destroy my soul with the ungodly
nor my life with bloodthirsty men,

in whose hands are evil devices and whose
right hands are full of bribes.

But as for me, I have walked in my
innocence; redeem me and have mercy
on me.

My foot has stood firm on the righteous
path; I will bless You, O Lord, in the
congregation.

PSALM 27 (26)

The Lord is my light and my salvation;
whom shall I fear?

The Lord is the defender of my life; of
whom shall I be afraid?

When evildoers assailed me to eat up
my flesh, my adversaries and foes, they
stumbled and fell.

Though an army encamp against me, my
heart shall not fear; though war rise up
against me, yet I am confident in this.

One thing have I asked of the Lord—that will I seek after—

that I may dwell in the house of the Lord all the days of my life, to behold the beauty of the Lord and to look upon His temple.

For He hid me in His shelter in the day of my afflictions;

He concealed me in the cover of His tabernacle; He set me high upon a rock.

And now, behold, my head has been lifted up above my enemies;

I will go round and offer in His tabernacle the sacrifice of joy; I will sing psalms and make melody to the Lord.

Hear my voice, O Lord, when I cry aloud; have mercy on me and answer me!

My heart said to You, "I have earnestly sought Your Face; Your Face, O Lord, will I seek."

Turn not Your Face away from me; do not turn away from your servant in anger.

Be my helper, forsake me not, and do not overlook me, O God my Savior!

For my father and my mother have forsaken me, but the Lord has taken me to Himself.

Instruct me in Your way, O Lord, and lead
me on a right path because of my enemies.

Give me not up to the will of my
oppressors; for false witnesses have risen
against me, and wicked men have lied to
themselves.

I believe that I shall see the goodness of the
Lord in the land of the living.

Wait on the Lord; be courageous and let
your heart be strengthened; yes, wait on
the Lord.

✠ ✠ ✠

KATHISMA 4—STASIS II

PSALM 28 (27)

To You, O Lord, will I call; O my God, be
not silent to me.

May You never be silent to me, lest I
become like those who go down to the pit.

Hear the voice of my supplication as I pray
to You, as I lift up my hands toward Your
holy temple.

Take me not away with sinners, and do not
destroy me with those who are workers of
iniquity,
who speak peace with their neighbors while
evils are in their hearts.
Requite them according to their work, and
according to the evil of their deeds;
requite them according to the work of their
hands; render them their due reward.
Because they do not regard Your works,
O Lord, nor the work of Your hands,
You will break them down and build them
up no more.
Blessed be the Lord! For He has heard the
voice of my supplication.
The Lord is my helper and my defender; in
Him my heart hopes, and so I am helped.
My flesh has revived, and I willingly give
praise to Him.
The Lord is the strength of His people and
the saving defender of His Anointed.
O Lord, save Your people and bless Your
inheritance: be their shepherd and lift
them up forever!

Offer to the Lord, O you sons of God, offer
young rams to the Lord! Ascribe to the
Lord glory and honor.

Offer to the Lord the glory due His name;
worship the Lord in His holy court.

The voice of the Lord is upon the waters;
the God of glory thunders; the Lord,
upon many waters!

The voice of the Lord is powerful; the voice
of the Lord is full of majesty.

The voice of the Lord breaks the cedars; the
Lord will break the cedars of Lebanon.

He will tear them in pieces, even the calf of
Lebanon; the beloved one is like a young
wild bull.

The voice of the Lord divides the flames
of fire; the voice of the Lord shakes
the wilderness; the Lord will shake the
wilderness of Kadesh.

The voice of the Lord strengthens the
hinds and will strip the forest bare; in His
temple everyone speaks of His glory.

The Lord sits enthroned over the flood; the
Lord will sit enthroned as King forever.

The Lord will give strength to His people;
the Lord will bless His people with peace!

PSALM 30 (29)

I will extol You, O Lord, for You have
drawn me up and have not caused my foes
to rejoice over me.

O Lord my God, I cried to You, and You
healed me.

O Lord, You have brought up my soul from
Sheol, restored me to life from among
those gone down to the pit.

Sing to the Lord, O you His saints, and
give thanks for the remembrance of His
holiness.

For there is destruction in His anger, but
life in His will.

Weeping shall tarry for the night, but joy
shall be in the morning.

As for me, I said in my prosperity, "I shall
never be moved."

O Lord, in Your good pleasure you added
strength to my beauty; but You hid Your
Face, and I was dismayed.

To You, O Lord, I cry; to my God I make
   supplication:
"What profit is there in my blood when I go
   down to destruction?
Will the dust praise You? Or will it declare
   Your truth?"
The Lord heard and had compassion on me;
   the Lord has become my helper.
You have turned for me my mourning
   into joy;
You have torn off my sackcloth and girded
   me with gladness,
that my glory may sing praise to You and
   that I may not be pierced with sorrow.
O Lord my God, I will give thanks to You
   forever!

✠ ✠ ✠

KATHISMA 4—STASIS III

PSALM 31 (30)

In You, O Lord, do I hope; let me never
   be put to shame; deliver me in Your
   righteousness and rescue me!

Incline Your ear to me; rescue me speedily!

Be a protecting God for me, a house of
refuge to save me!

You are my strength and my refuge; for
Your name's sake You will guide me and
keep me.

You will take me out of the net which is
hidden for me, for You, O Lord, are my
defender.

Into Your hands I commit my spirit; You
have redeemed me, O Lord, God of truth.

You have hated those who idly persist in
vanities; but I have hoped in the Lord.

I will rejoice and be glad in Your mercy,
because You have seen my affliction;

You have saved my soul from adversities
and have not delivered me into the hand
of the enemy; You have set my feet in a
broad place.

Have mercy on me, O Lord, for I am
afflicted; my eye is wasted from
indignation, my soul and my body also.

For my life is spent with sorrow and my
years with sighing.

My strength fails because of my poverty,
and my bones waste away.

I have become a reproach among all my
adversaries, a horror to my neighbors, an
object of dread to my acquaintances;

those who saw me in the street fled
from me.

I have passed out of mind like one who is
dead; I have become like a broken vessel.

For I heard the slander of many that live on
every side: they gathered together against
me as they plotted to take away my life.

But I hoped in You, O Lord: I said, "You are
my God. My lots are in Your hand."

Deliver me from the hand of my enemies
and persecutors.

Let Your Face shine on Your servant; save
me in Your mercy!

Let me not be put to shame, O Lord, for
I call on You; let the ungodly be put to
shame and brought down to Sheol.

Let the lying lips be dumb which speak
insolently against the righteous in pride
and contempt.

How abundant is the multitude of Your
goodness, which You have laid up for
those who fear You and wrought for those
who hope in You, in the presence of the
sons of men!

In the secret place of Your presence You
will hide them from the plots of men;

You will hold them safe in Your tabernacle
from the strife of tongues.

Blessed be the Lord, for He has worked
wonders of mercy for me in a
fortified city.

But I said in my alarm, "I am driven far
from the sight of Your eyes."

Therefore You heard the voice of my
supplications when I cried to You.

Love the Lord, all you His saints, for the
Lord seeks for truth and abundantly
requites those who act haughtily.

Take courage and let your heart be
strengthened, all who hope in the Lord!

PSALM 32 (31)

Blessed is he whose transgression is
forgiven, whose sin is covered.

Blessed is the man to whom the Lord
imputes no iniquity and in whose mouth
there is no deceit.

When I declared not my sin, my body
wasted away through my groaning all
day long.

For day and night Your hand was heavy
upon me; my strength was dried up as by
the heat of summer.

I acknowledged my sin to You, and I did not
hide my iniquity.

I said, "I will confess my transgressions
to the Lord"; then You forgave the
ungodliness of my heart.

For his sin, everyone who is godly will offer
prayer to You at a fitting time; and the
rush of great waters shall not reach him.

You are my hiding place from the affliction
that surrounds me; my joy, to deliver me
from those who encompass me.

"I will instruct you and teach you the
way you should go; I will set my eyes
upon you."

Be not like a horse or a mule, without
understanding, which must be curbed

with bit and bridle, or else it will not
keep with you.

Many are the pangs of the wicked; but
mercy surrounds him who trusts in
the Lord.

Be glad in the Lord and rejoice,
O righteous, and shout for joy, all you
upright in heart!

✠ ✠ ✠

KATHISMA 5—STASIS I

PSALM 33 (32)

Rejoice in the Lord, O you righteous!
Praise befits the just.

Praise the Lord with the lyre; make a
melody to Him with the harp of ten
strings!

Sing to Him a new song; sing praises
beautifully with a loud shout.

For the word of the Lord is right, and all
His works are faithfulness.

He loves mercy and judgment; the earth is
full of the mercy of the Lord.

By the Word of the Lord the heavens were
made, and all their host by the Spirit of
His mouth.

He gathers the waters of the sea as in a
bottle; He put the deeps in storehouses.

Let all the earth fear the Lord; let all
the inhabitants of the world be moved
because of Him!

For He spoke and they were made; He
commanded and they were created.

The Lord frustrates the counsel of the
nations; He brings to naught the plans of
the people and the reasoning of princes.

But the counsel of the Lord stands forever,
the thoughts of His heart from generation
to generation.

Blessed is the nation whose God is the Lord,
the people whom He has chosen for His
own inheritance!

The Lord looked down from heaven and
saw all the sons of men;

He looks from His prepared habitation on
all the inhabitants of the earth:

He who alone fashions their hearts and
observes all their deeds.

A king is not saved by his great army;
a giant is not delivered by his great
strength.

The war horse is a vain hope for victory;
despite its great might, it cannot save.

Behold, the eyes of the Lord are on those
who fear Him, on those who hope in His
mercy,

that He may deliver their soul from death,
and keep them alive in famine.

Our soul waits for the Lord; He is our
helper and defender.

Our heart shall rejoice in Him, and we have
hoped in His holy name.

Let Your mercy, O Lord, be upon us, as we
have set our hope on You.

PSALM 34 (33)

I will bless the Lord at all times; His praise
shall continually be in my mouth.

My soul makes its boast in the Lord; let the
meek hear and be glad.

O magnify the Lord with me, and let us
exalt His name together!

I sought the Lord with diligence, and He
heard me and delivered me from all my
tribulations.

Draw near to Him and be illumined, so
your faces shall not be ashamed.

This poor man cried and the Lord heard
him, and saved him out of all his troubles.

The angel of the Lord will encamp
around those who fear Him and will
deliver them.

O taste and see that the Lord is good!
Blessed is the man who hopes in Him!

O fear the Lord, all you His saints, for those
who fear Him have no want!

The rich have become poor and hungry; but
those who seek the Lord with diligence
shall lack no good thing.

Come, O sons, listen to me; I will teach you
the fear of the Lord.

What man is there who desires life, loving
to see good days?

Keep your tongue from evil and your lips
from speaking deceit.

Depart from evil and do good; seek peace
and pursue it.

The eyes of the Lord are upon the
righteous, and His ears are open to their
supplication.

But the Face of the Lord is against evildoers
to cut off the remembrance of them from
the earth.

The righteous called, and the Lord heard
them and delivered them out of all their
afflictions.

The Lord is near to the brokenhearted and
saves the lowly in spirit.

Many are the afflictions of the righteous,
but the Lord delivers them out of
them all.

He keeps all his bones; not one of them
shall be broken.

The death of sinners is wretched, and those
who hate righteousness will stumble.

The Lord will redeem the souls of His
servants; none of those who hope in Him
will stumble.

✠ ✠ ✠

KATHISMA 5—STASIS II

PSALM 35 (34)

Judge, O Lord, those who wrong me; fight
against those who fight against me.

Take hold of shield and buckler and rise for
my help.
Draw the sword and stop the way against
those who persecute me.
Say to my soul, "I am your salvation."
Let those be put to shame and confounded
who seek after my soul.
Let those who desire evil for me be turned
back and brought to dishonor.
Let them be as dust before the wind, with
the angel of the Lord afflicting them.
Let their way be dark and slippery, with the
angel of the Lord pursuing them.
For without cause they hid their snare for
me; without cause they have reproached
my soul.
Let a snare come upon them unawares! Let
the net which they hid take them, and let
them fall into the same snare.
Then my soul shall rejoice in the Lord,
exulting in His salvation.
All my bones shall say, "O Lord, who is
like You, delivering the poor out of the
hand of those who are stronger than he,

the poor and the needy from those who despoil him?"

False witnesses rose up and asked me of things I knew not.

They rewarded me evil for good; my soul is forlorn.

But I, when they troubled me, put on sackcloth and humbled my soul with fasting; I prayed with my head bowed down.

I behaved agreeably toward them as though to our neighbor or brother.

I humbled myself as one sad of countenance and in mourning.

But they rejoiced at my expense; they gathered together against me.

Many whips came down on me, and I knew not why.

They tempted me; they mocked me with contempt, gnashing at me with their teeth.

They were scattered, but they did not repent.

O Lord, when will You look on me? Deliver my soul from their mischief, my life from the lions!

Then I will confess You in the great congregation; in the mighty throng I will praise You.

Let not those rejoice over me who are my enemies without a cause,

those who hate me without reason and wink to one another with the eye.

For they spoke peace to me; but in their fury, they conceived words of deceit.

They opened wide their mouths against me; they said, "Aha, aha, our eyes have seen his downfall."

You have seen, O Lord; be not silent!
O Lord, be not far from me!

Awake, O Lord, and attend to my judgment, to my cause, my God and my Lord.

Judge me, O Lord, according to Your righteousness, and let them rejoice no longer at my expense.

Let them not say in their hearts anymore, "Aha, we have our heart's desire!"

Let them not say anymore, "We have
swallowed him up."

Let them be put to shame and confusion
altogether who rejoice at my calamity.

Let them be clothed with shame and
dishonor who magnify themselves
against me.

Let those who rejoice in my righteousness
shout for joy and be glad and say
evermore,

"Great is the Lord, who delights in the
peace of His servant!"

Then my tongue shall tell of Your
righteousness and of Your praise all the
day long.

PSALM 36 (35)

The transgressor has resolved to sin; there
is no fear of God before his eyes.

For he deals craftily with himself, so that he
may not find out his iniquity and hate it.

The words of his mouth are mischief and
deceit; he is not inclined to act wisely and
do good.

He plots mischief while on his bed; he
sets himself in a way that is not good; he
spurns not evil.

Your mercy, O Lord, extends to the
heavens, Your truth to the clouds.

Your righteousness is like the mountains of
God; Your judgments are like the great
deep; O Lord, You will save men and
beasts.

How You have multiplied Your mercy,
O God! The sons of men take refuge in
the shadow of Your wings.

They feast on the abundance of Your house,
and You give them drink from the river
of Your delights.

For with You is the fountain of life; in Your
light we shall see light.

Continue Your mercy on those who know
You, and Your righteousness to the
upright of heart!

Let not the foot of the arrogant come upon
me, nor the hand of the wicked drive
me away.

There the evildoers lie prostrate; they are
cast out, unable to rise.

✠ ✠ ✠

KATHISMA 5—STASIS III

PSALM 37 (36)

Be not jealous of the wicked nor envious of
evildoers.

For they will soon fade like the grass and
wither like the green herb.

Hope in the Lord and do good; so you will
dwell in the land and be fed with its
wealth.

Take delight in the Lord, and He will give
you the desires of your heart.

Disclose your struggles to the Lord; hope in
Him, and He will act.

He will cause your righteousness to shine
forth as the light and your judgment as
the noonday.

Be still before the Lord and submit yourself
to Him;

be not jealous of him who prospers in his
way, of the man who transgresses the law.

Refrain from anger, and forsake wrath. Let
   not envy lead you to evil deeds.

For the wicked shall be cut off; but those
   who wait for the Lord shall possess
   the land.

Yet a little while, and the wicked will be no
   more; though you look well at his place,
   he will not be there.

But the meek shall inherit the earth and
   delight themselves in the fullness of
   peace.

The sinner will plot against the righteous
   and gnash his teeth at him;

but the Lord shall laugh at him, for He sees
   that his day is coming.

The wicked have drawn their swords and
   bent their bows to bring down the poor
   and needy, to slay the upright in heart.

Let their sword enter their own heart and
   their bows be broken.

Better is the little the righteous has than the
   great wealth of sinners.

For the arms of the wicked shall be broken,
   but the Lord upholds the righteous.

The Lord knows the days of the blameless,
and their heritage will abide forever.

They are not put to shame in evil times; in
the days of famine they have abundance.

But the wicked perish; the enemies of the
Lord, at the moment of being honored
and exalted, like smoke they vanish away.

The wicked borrows and will not pay back,
but the righteous has compassion and
gives;

for those who bless the Lord shall possess
the land, but those who curse Him shall
be cut off.

The Lord guides the steps of man, and He
will delight in his ways.

Though he fall, he shall not be cast
headlong, for the Lord is the stay of
his hand.

I have been young and now am old,

yet I have not seen the righteous forsaken or
his children begging bread.

He is merciful and ever lending, and his
children shall be blessed.

Depart from evil and do good; so shall you
abide forever.

For the Lord loves justice; He will not
forsake His saints; they shall be preserved
forever.

The sinners will be chastised, and the
children of the ungodly shall be
destroyed;

but the righteous shall inherit the earth and
dwell upon it forever.

The mouth of the righteous will meditate
on wisdom, and his tongue will speak
justice.

The law of his God is in his heart, and his
steps will not slip.

The wicked watches the righteous and seeks
to slay him.

The Lord will not abandon him into his
hands or let him be condemned when he
is brought to trial.

Wait for the Lord and keep to His way, and
He will exalt you to possess the land;

you will look on the destruction of the
wicked.

I have seen a wicked man overbearing and
towering like a cedar of Lebanon.

Again I passed by, and lo, he was no more;
though I sought him, he could not be
found.

Maintain innocence and behold
uprightness, for there is posterity for the
man of peace.

But transgressors shall be altogether
destroyed; the posterity of the ungodly
shall be cut off.

The salvation of the righteous is from the
Lord; He is their defender in the time of
tribulation;

the Lord shall help them and deliver them;
He shall deliver them from the wicked
and save them, because they have hoped
in Him.

✠ ✠ ✠

Monday—Vespers

PSALM 38 (37)

O Lord, rebuke me not in Your anger, nor
chasten me in Your wrath.

For Your arrows have sunk into me, and
Your hand has come down on me.

There is no soundness in my flesh because
of Your indignation; there is no health in
my bones because of my sins.

For my iniquities have gone over my head;
they weigh like a burden too heavy
for me.

My wounds grow foul and fester because
of my foolishness; I am utterly bowed
down and prostrate; all the day I go about
mourning.

For my soul is filled with burning, and
there is no soundness in my flesh.

I am utterly spent and crushed; I groan
because of the tumult of my heart.

O Lord, all my longing is known to You; my
sighing is not hidden from You.

My heart throbs, my strength fails me, and the light of my eyes—it also has gone from me.

My friends and companions stand aloof from my plague, and my kinsmen stand afar off.

Those who seek my life lay their snares; those who seek my hurt speak of ruin and meditate treachery all the day long.

But I am like a deaf man; I do not hear, like a dumb man who does not open his mouth.

I am like a man who does not hear and in whose mouth are no rebukes.

But in You, O Lord, have I hoped; You, O Lord my God, will answer.

For I pray, "Only let them not rejoice over me," who boast against me when my foot slips.

For I am ready to fall, and my pain is ever with me. I confess my iniquity; I am sorry for my sin.

But those who are my foes without cause are mighty, and many are those who hate me wrongfully.

Those who render me evil for good are my adversaries, because I follow after good.

Do not forsake me, O Lord! O my God, be not far from me! Make haste to help me, O Lord, my salvation!

PSALM 39 (38)

I said, "I will take heed to my ways, that I may not sin with my tongue";

I set a guard on my mouth so long as the sinner stood in my presence.

I was dumb and humbled myself and kept silence even from good words, but my grief was renewed.

My heart became hot within me; a fire kindled in my meditation; then I spoke with my tongue:

Lord, let me know my end and what is the measure of my days, that I may know what I lack.

Behold, you have made my days a few handbreadths, and my lifetime is as nothing in Your sight.

No, every man living is altogether vanity! Surely man goes about as a shadow!

Surely for naught are they in turmoil; man heaps up treasures and knows not for whom he gathers them.

And now, for what do I wait? Is it not the Lord? Even my existence is from you.

Deliver me from all my transgressions; You have made me the scorn of the fool.

I was dumb; I did not open my mouth, for this was from You.

Remove Your stroke from me; I am spent by the blows of Your hand.

In chastening man for his sin, You instruct him.

You make his life to be consumed like a spider's web; yes, every man is in turmoil for nothing.

Hear my prayer, O Lord, and give ear to my cry; hold not Your peace at my tears!

For I am Your passing guest, a sojourner, like all my fathers.

Spare me, that I may find the place of refreshment before I depart and am no more!

I waited eagerly for the Lord, and He
   inclined to me and heard my cry.

He brought me up out of a pit of misery
   and from miry clay and ordered my way
   aright.

He put a new song in my mouth, a song of
   praise to our God.

Many will see and fear and put their trust
   in the Lord.

Blessed is the man whose hope is in the
   name of the Lord, who has not turned to
   vanities, to that which deceives and leads
   astray!

You have multiplied, O Lord my God, Your
   wondrous deeds, and in Your thoughts
   none can compare with You!

I proclaimed and told of them; they were
   more than can be numbered.

Sacrifice and offering You do not desire, but
   You have prepared a body for me;

burnt offering and sin offering, You have
   not required; so then I said, "Lo, I come."

In the roll of the book it is written of me: I delight to do Your will, O my God; Your law is within my heart.

I have proclaimed Your righteousness in the great congregation;

lo, I will not restrain my lips, as You know, O Lord.

I have not hidden Your truth within my heart; I have spoken of Your salvation.

I have not concealed Your mercy and Your truth from the great congregation.

O Lord, do not withhold Your mercy from me; Your mercy and Your truth have ever preserved me.

For evils have encompassed me without number; my iniquities have overtaken me till I cannot see;

they are more than the hairs of my head; my heart fails me.

Be pleased, O Lord, to deliver me; O Lord, make haste to help me!

Let those be put to shame and confusion who seek my life!

Let those who desire evil for me be turned back and brought to dishonor.

Let those who say, "Aha, aha!" be put to
confusion.

Let all who seek You rejoice and be glad in
You! Let those who love Your salvation
say evermore, "God is great!"

But I am poor and needy; hasten to me,
O God! You are my help and deliverer;
O Lord, do not delay.

✠ ✠ ✠

KATHISMA 6—STASIS II

PSALM 41 (40)

Blessed is He who considers the poor and
needy! The Lord will deliver Him in the
day of trouble.

The Lord will protect him and keep him
alive, and bless him on the earth, and not
deliver him into the hands of his enemy.

The Lord will sustain him on his sickbed;
from his illness and all his infirmities,
You will heal him.

I said, "Lord, have mercy on me; heal my soul, for I have sinned against You."

My enemies say of me in malice, "When will he die and his name perish?"

And if one came to see me, he uttered empty words;

his heart gathered iniquity; when he goes out, he tells it abroad.

All my enemies whispered together about me; they devised evil against me. They uttered lawless words against me.

But He who fell asleep, will he not rise again?

For even the man to whom I had given my peace, in whom I trusted—

he who ate of my bread has lifted his heel against me.

But O Lord, have compassion on me and raise me up, and I shall requite them!

By this I know that You have delighted in me, because my enemy shall not rejoice over me.

But You have upheld me because of my innocence and set me before Your Face forever.

Blessed be the Lord, the God of Israel, from
everlasting to everlasting! Amen and
Amen.

PSALM 42 (41)

As a hart longs for flowing streams, so
longs my soul for You, O God.
My soul thirsts for God, for the living God.
When shall I come and behold the Face
of God?
My tears have been my food day and night,
while men say to me continually, "Where
is your God?"
These things I remembered as I poured out
my soul:
Yes, I will go to the place of Your wonderful
tabernacle, even to the house of God,
with glad shouts and songs of thanksgiving
of a multitude keeping festival.
Why are you cast down, O my soul, and
why are you disquieted within me?
Hope in God; for I will give thanks to Him,
the salvation of my countenance and
my God.

My soul is cast down within me; therefore,
I have remembered You from the land of
Jordan and of Hermon, from the small
mountain.

Deep calls to deep at the thunder of Your
cataracts; all Your waves and your billows
have gone over me.

By day the Lord will command His mercy;
by night I will sing a psalm to Him—a
prayer to the God of my life.

I will say to God, "You are my Helper; why
have You forgotten me?"

Why do I go mourning because of the
oppression of the enemy?

While my bones were breaking, my
adversaries taunted me, while they said to
me daily, "Where is your God?"

Why are you cast down, O my soul, and
why are you disquieted within me?

Hope in God, for I will give thanks to Him,
the help of my countenance and my God.

Judge me, O God, and defend my cause
   against an ungodly people; from the
   deceitful and unjust man deliver me!

For You, O God, are my strength; why have
   You cast me off?

Why do I go mourning because of the
   oppression of the enemy?

O Lord, send out Your light and Your truth;

let them lead me; let them bring me to Your
   holy mountain and to Your tabernacle!

And I will go to the altar of God, to God
   the joy of my youth;

I will give thanks to You with the lyre,
   O God, my God.

Why are you cast down, O my soul, and
   why are you disquieted within me?

Hope in God; for I shall again praise Him,
   my help and my God.

✠ ✠ ✠

PSALM 44 (43)

We have heard with our ears, O God,
   and our fathers have told us what deeds
   You performed in their days, in the days
   of old:
With Your own hand You drove out the
   nations, but You planted our fathers;
You afflicted the peoples and cast them out.
For not by their own sword did they
   win the land; nor did their own arm
   save them,
but Your right hand and Your arm and
   the light of Your countenance; for You
   delighted in them.
You are my King and my God who
   commands deliverance for Jacob.
Through You we push down our foes;
   through Your name we tread down our
   assailants.
For not in my bow do I trust, nor will my
   sword save me.

For You have saved us from those who
 oppose us and have put to shame those
 who hate us.

In God will we make our boast all the day,
 and we will give thanks to Your name
 forever.

But now You have cast us off; You have
 covered us with shame; You do not go out
 any longer with our armies.

You have made us flee before our foes; and
 those who hated us have gotten spoil.

You have made us like sheep for slaughter,
 and have scattered us among the nations.

You have sold Your people for no price, and
 there was no profit in their exchange.

You have made us the taunt of our
 neighbors, the derision and scorn of those
 about us.

You have made us a byword among the
 nations, a laughingstock among the
 peoples.

All day long my disgrace is before me, and
 shame has covered my face

at the voice of the slanderer and reviler,
 because of the enemy and the avenger.

All this has come upon us, though we
   have not forgotten You or betrayed Your
   covenant.
And our heart has not turned back, but
   You have turned our steps aside from
   Your way,
for You have laid us low in a place of
   affliction, and the shadow of death has
   covered us.
If we had forgotten the name of our God or
   spread forth our hands to a strange god,
would not God have discovered this? For
   He knows the secrets of the heart.
No, for Your sake we are slain all the day
   long and accounted as sheep for the
   slaughter.
Awake! Why do You sleep, O Lord? Arise,
   and do not cast us off forever!
Why do You hide Your Face? Why do You
   forget our poverty and affliction?
For our soul has been bowed down to the
   dust; our body cleaves to the ground.
Arise, O Lord, and help us! Deliver us for
   Your name's sake!

My heart overflows with a goodly theme; I
address my verses to the king; my tongue
is like the pen of a ready scribe.

You are the fairest of the sons of men; grace
is poured upon Your lips; therefore God
has blessed you forever.

Gird your sword upon Your thigh, O
Mighty One, in Your glory and majesty.

Draw Your bow; ride forth in triumph, and
reign for the sake of truth and meekness
and righteousness.

May Your right hand teach You dread deeds!

Your arrows are sharp in the heart of
the king's enemies; the peoples fall
under You.

Your throne, O God, endures forever and
ever; the scepter of righteousness is the
scepter of Your Kingdom.

You love righteousness and hate iniquity;
therefore, God, Your God, has anointed
You with the oil of gladness above Your
fellows.

Your robes are all fragrant with myrrh and
aloes and cassia.

From ivory palaces, stringed instruments
  make You glad; daughters of kings are
  among Your ladies of honor; at Your right
  hand stands the queen in gold of Ophir.

Hear, O daughter, and see and incline your
  ear; forget your people and your father's
  house;

then the King will desire your beauty,
  for He is your Lord, and you shall
  worship Him.

And the people of Tyre come with gifts;
  even the rich among the people shall seek
  your favor.

The King's daughter is all glorious within;
  her robes are of cloth of gold.

Clad in many colors she is led to the King:
  after her, the virgins, her companions, are
  brought to You.

They are led in with joy and gladness; they
  enter the temple of the King.

Instead of your fathers, sons are born to
  you; you shall make them princes over all
  the earth.

I will cause your name to be celebrated in
all generations; therefore the peoples shall
praise you forever and ever.

PSALM 46 (45)

God is our refuge and strength, a help in
the afflictions that have come upon us.

Therefore we will not fear if the earth be
shaken, if the mountains are removed to
the heart of the sea; if their waters roar
and are troubled, and if the mountains are
shaken by His might.

There is a river whose streams make glad
the city of God; the Most High has
sanctified His tabernacle.

God is in the midst of her; she shall not
be moved; God will help her with His
countenance.

The nations were troubled, the kingdoms
tottered; He uttered His voice, the earth
shook.

The Lord of hosts is with us; the God of
Jacob is our refuge.

Come, behold the works of the Lord, what
wonders He has wrought on the earth.

He makes wars cease to the end of the earth;
He will break the bow and shatter the
spear and burn the shield with fire!

Be still and know that I am God. I am
exalted among the nations; I am exalted in
the earth!

The Lord of hosts is with us; the God of
Jacob is our refuge.

✠ ✠ ✠

PSALM 47 (46)

Clap your hands, all peoples! Shout to God
with loud songs of joy!

For the Lord, the Most High, is terrible, a
great King over all the earth.

He subdues peoples under us and nations
under our feet.

He has chosen His inheritance for us: the
beauty of Jacob whom He loved.

God has gone up with a shout, the Lord
with the sound of a trumpet!

Sing praises to our God, sing praises! Sing
praises to our King, sing praises!

For God is the king of all the earth; sing
praises with wisdom!

God reigns over the nations; God sits on the
throne of His holiness.

The rulers of the people are assembled with
the God of Abraham,

for God's mighty ones on earth have been
greatly exalted!

PSALM 48 (47)

Great is the Lord, and greatly to be praised,
  in the city of our God and on His holy
  mountain;
He founded it for the joy of all the earth:
  Mount Zion, the city of the great King.
Within her citadels God is known when He
  defends her.
For lo, the kings assembled, they came on
  together.
They saw and they wondered; they were
  troubled, they were moved.
Trembling took hold of them there, pangs as
  of a woman in travail.
By a vehement wind You broke the ships of
  Tarshish.
As we have heard, so have we seen, in the
  city of the Lord of hosts, in the city of
  our God. God has established her forever.
We have thought of Your mercy, O God, in
  the midst of Your people.
As Your name, O God, so Your praise
  reaches to the ends of the earth.
Your right hand is filled with righteousness;
  let Mount Zion be glad!

Let the daughters of Judah rejoice because
of Your judgments, O Lord!

Walk about Zion, go round about her,
number her towers,

let your hearts consider well her strength,
observe her citadels,

so that you may proclaim to the coming
generations that the Lord is our God
forever and ever;

He is our shepherd for all eternity.

PSALM 49 (48)

Hear this, all peoples! Give ear, all
inhabitants of the world!

Both sons of low men and sons of high, rich
and poor together!

My mouth shall speak wisdom; the
meditation of my heart shall be
understanding.

I will incline my ear to a proverb; I will
solve my riddle in psalmody.

Why should I fear in times of trouble,
when the iniquity of my persecutors
surrounds me,

men who trust in their power and boast of
the abundance of their riches?

Their brother was not able to redeem them;
shall a man redeem them?

He will not give to God a ransom for
Himself, nor the price of the redemption
of His own soul;

He will labor in this age and live forever,
for He will not see corruption,

while He shall see even the wise die; the
fool and the stupid alike must perish and
leave their wealth to strangers.

Their graves will be their homes forever,
their dwelling places to all generations,
though they called lands after their own
names.

Man, when he was honored, did not
understand, but ranked himself with
senseless beasts and became like them.

Their way will be the cause of their fall,
though afterward men will commend
their sayings.

Like sheep they are appointed for Sheol;
death shall be their shepherd;

but God will deliver my soul from the grasp
of Sheol when He will receive me.

Be not afraid when one becomes rich, when
the glory of his house increases.

For when he dies he will carry nothing
away; his glory will not go down
after him.

Though while he lives, a man receives
flattery, and though he acknowledges You
when You grant him prosperity,

he will go to the generation of his fathers;
he will never more see the light.

Man, when he was honored, did not
understand, but ranked himself with
senseless beasts and became like them.

☩ ☩ ☩

KATHISMA 7—STASIS II

PSALM 50 (49)

The Lord, the God of gods, speaks and
summons the earth from the rising of the
sun to its setting.

Out of Zion shines forth the perfection of
His beauty.

God, our God, shall come openly and shall
not keep silence.

A fire shall be kindled before Him; round
about Him shall be a mighty tempest.

He shall call to the heavens above and to the
earth, that He may judge His people:

Gather to Me, my venerable ones, who
made a covenant with Me by sacrifice!

The heavens shall declare His righteousness,
for God Himself is judge.

Hear, O my people, and I will speak to you,
O Israel. I will testify to you: I am God,
your God.

I will not reprove you for your sacrifices;
your burnt offerings are continually
before me.

I will accept no bull from your house nor
he-goat from your folds.

For all the wild beasts of the forest are
mine, the cattle on the hills and the oxen.

I know all the birds of the air, and the
beauty of the field is mine.

If I should be hungry, I will not tell you, for the world is mine and all its fullness.

Will I eat the flesh of bulls or drink the blood of goats?

Offer to God the sacrifice of praise, and pay your vows to the Most High,

and call upon Me in the day of trouble; I will deliver you, and you shall glorify Me.

But to the sinner God has said, "Why do you recite my statutes, or take my covenant in your mouth?

For you have hated discipline, and have cast My words behind you.

If you saw a thief, you ran along with him, and you cast your lot with adulterers.

Your mouth has multiplied wickedness, and your tongue has framed deceit.

You sat and spoke against your brother; you slandered your mother's son.

These things you have done, and I have been silent; you thought wickedly that I should be one like yourself.

But I will rebuke you and lay the charge before you.

Mark these things, then, you who forget
  God, lest I rend and there be no deliverer!
The sacrifice of praise will glorify Me; there
  I will show him the salvation of God!"

PSALM 51 (50)

Have mercy on me, O God, according to
  Your steadfast love;
according to your abundant mercy, blot out
  my transgressions.
Wash me thoroughly from my iniquity and
  cleanse me from my sin.
For I know my transgressions, and my sin is
  ever before me.
Against You, You only, have I sinned and
  done that which is evil in Your sight,
so that You are justified in Your sentence
  and blameless in Your judgment.
Behold, I was brought forth in iniquity, and
  in sin did my mother conceive me.
Behold, You desire truth in the inward
  being; therefore, teach me wisdom in my
  secret heart.
Purge me with hyssop, and I shall be clean;
  wash me, and I shall be whiter than snow.

Fill me with joy and gladness; let the bones
which You have broken rejoice.

Hide Your Face from my sins and blot out
all my iniquities.

Create in me a clean heart, O God, and put
a new and right spirit within me.

Cast me not away from Your presence, and
take not Your Holy Spirit from me.

Restore to me the joy of Your salvation, and
uphold me with a willing spirit.

Then I will teach transgressors Your ways,
and sinners will return to You.

Deliver me from bloodguilt, O God, God
of my salvation, and my tongue will sing
aloud of Your deliverance.

O Lord, open my lips, and my mouth shall
show forth Your praise.

For You have no delight in sacrifice; were I
to give a burnt offering, You would not be
pleased.

The sacrifice acceptable to God is a broken
spirit; a broken and contrite heart,
O God, You will not despise.

Do good to Zion in Your good pleasure;
rebuild the walls of Jerusalem;

then will You delight in right sacrifices, in
burnt offerings and whole burnt offerings;
then bulls will be offered on Your altar.

✠ ✠ ✠

KATHISMA 7—STASIS III

PSALM 52 (51)

Why do you glory in your evil, O mighty
man?

All the day your tongue is plotting
unrighteousness; like a sharp razor, you
have worked treachery.

You have loved evil more than good,
and wickedness more than speaking
righteousness.

You love all words of destruction,
O deceitful tongue.

Therefore, may God break you down
forever; may He snatch and tear you from
your dwelling and uproot you from the
land of the living.

The righteous shall see and fear and shall
laugh at him, saying,

"See the man who would not make God his
   help, but trusted in the abundance of his
   riches and strengthened himself in his
   vanity."
But I am like a green olive tree in the house
   of God.
I have trusted in the mercy of God forever
   and ever.
I will give thanks to You forever, because
   You have done it.
I will wait upon Your name, for it is good,
   in the presence of the saints.

PSALM 53 (52)

The fool says in his heart, "There is
   no God."
They are corrupt; they do abominable
   deeds; there is none who does good.
God looked down from heaven and saw
   all the sons of men, to see if there are
   any that have understood, that sought
   after God.
They have all fallen away; they are all alike
   unprofitable; there is none that does good,
   no, not one.

Shall they never learn, those who practice
lawlessness, those who eat up my people
as they eat bread? They do not call
upon God.

There they were in great terror, where there
was no cause for fear,

for God has scattered the bones of the men-
pleasers; they were ashamed, for God has
rejected them.

Who will bring about the salvation of Israel
out of Zion?

When God brings back the captives of
His people, Jacob will rejoice and Israel
be glad.

PSALM 54 (53)

Save me, O God, by Your name and judge
me by Your strength.

Hear my prayer, O God; give ear to the
words of my mouth.

For insolent men have risen against me;
ruthless men seek my life; they do not set
God before them.

Behold, God is my helper; the Lord is the
protector of my soul.

He will requite my enemies with evil; in
　　Your truth put an end to them.
Voluntarily I will sacrifice to You; I will
　　give thanks to Your name, O Lord, for it
　　is good.
For You have delivered me from every
　　trouble, and my eye has looked in
　　triumph on my enemies!

PSALM 55 (54)

Give ear to my prayer, O God, and hide not
　　Yourself from my supplication!
Attend to me and answer me; I am grieved
　　in my meditation and troubled because of
　　the noise of the enemy,
because of the oppression of the wicked.
For they bring trouble upon me, and in
　　anger they cherish enmity against me.
My heart is in anguish within me; the
　　terrors of death have fallen upon me.
Fear and trembling come upon me, and
　　horror overwhelms me.

And I say, "Oh, that I had wings like a dove!
    I would fly away and be at rest.
Yes, I would wander afar, I would lodge
    in the wilderness; I would hasten to
    find a shelter from the raging wind and
    tempest."
Destroy their plans, O Lord, confuse their
    tongues; for I see violence and strife in
    the city.
Day and night they go around it on its walls;
    and mischief and trouble are within it,
    ruin is in its midst;
oppression and fraud do not depart from its
    marketplace.
It is not an enemy who taunts me—then I
    could bear it;
it is not an adversary who deals insolently
    with me—then I could hide from him.
But it is you, my equal, my companion, my
    familiar friend.
We used to hold sweet converse together;
    within God's house we walked in
    fellowship.

Let death come upon them; let them go down to Sheol alive; let them go away in terror into their graves.

But I call upon God, and the Lord will save me.

Evening and morning and at noon I utter my complaint and moan, and He will hear my voice.

He will deliver my soul in safety from the battle that I wage, for many are arrayed against me.

God will give ear and humble them, He who is before all ages.

For they suffer no calamity and therefore do not fear God.

My companion stretched out his hand against his friends; he violated his covenant.

His speech was smoother than butter, yet war was in his heart;

his words were softer than oil, yet they were drawn swords.

Cast your burden on the Lord, and He will sustain you; He will never permit the righteous to be moved.

But You, O God, will cast them down into
the lowest pit; men of blood and treachery
shall not live out half their days.

But I will trust in You.

✠ ✠ ✠

KATHISMA 8—STASIS I

PSALM 56 (55)

Have mercy on me, O God, for man has trampled upon me; all day long my foe has oppressed me;

all day long my enemies trample upon me; many are those who fight against me.

In the light of day I will not fear, for I have placed my hope in the Lord.

In God, whose word I praise, all the day I have hoped in God; I will not fear what flesh will do to me.

All day long they slander my words; all their plots are against me for evil.

There they are; they lurk, they watch my steps; they lie in wait for my soul.

But You will not grant them victory; in Your wrath You will cast down the peoples, O God.

I have manifested my life to You; You have put my tears before You according to Your promise!

My enemies will be turned back in the day
when I call on You; lo, I know that You
are my God.

In God, whose word I praise, in the Lord,
whose word I praise, in God I have hoped.

I will not be afraid of what man will do
to me.

I will render to You, O God, the vows of
praise which are upon me.

For You have delivered my soul from death,
yes, my feet from falling, that I may be
well-pleasing before God in the land of
the living.

PSALM 57 (56)

Be merciful to me, O God, be merciful to
me, for my soul has trusted in You;

in the shadow of Your wings I will seek
refuge till the storms of lawlessness
pass by.

I will cry to God Most High, the God who
is my benefactor.

He sent from heaven and saved me. He put
to shame those who trampled upon me.

I lay down to sleep in torment, but God
sent forth His mercy and His truth and
delivered my soul from the midst of
young lions.

The sons of men, their teeth are spears and
arrows, their tongue a sharp sword.

Be exalted, O God, above the heavens, and
Your glory over all the earth!

They set a net for my steps; they bowed
down my soul.

They dug a pit before my face, but they fell
into it themselves.

My heart, O God, is ready, my heart is
ready. I will sing, yes, I will sing psalms!

Awake, O my soul! Awake, O harp and lyre!
I will awake the dawn!

I will confess You, O Lord, among the
peoples; I will sing praises to You among
the nations.

For Your mercy is higher than the heavens,
and Your truth reaches to the clouds.

Be exalted, O God, above the heavens, and
Your glory over all the earth!

Do you indeed judge according to
righteousness? Do you judge rightly,
O sons of men?

For in your hearts you work evils in the
earth; your hands weave unrighteousness.

The wicked have gone astray from the
womb; they err from their birth,
speaking lies.

Their anger is like that of the serpent, like
the deaf adder that stops its ear

so that it does not hear the voice of
enchanters or of the charm prepared
cunningly by the wise.

God has broken the teeth in their mouths;
God has torn out the fangs of the young
lions.

Let them vanish like water that runs away;
He shall bend His bow until they fail.

They shall be as melted wax; fire has come
down on them, and they no longer see
the sun.

Sooner than your thorns can feel the heat,
He will swallow you up alive in His
wrath!

The righteous will rejoice when he sees the vengeance on the ungodly; he will bathe his feet in the blood of the wicked.

A man will say, "Surely, then, there is a reward for the righteous; surely there is a God who judges them on earth."

☩ ☩ ☩

KATHISMA 8—STASIS II

PSALM 59 (58)

Deliver me from my enemies, O God; save me from those who rise up against me.

Deliver me from those who work evil, and save me from bloodthirsty men.

For lo, they have hunted for my soul;

fierce men have set upon me for no transgression or sin of mine, O Lord, for no fault of mine.

Without evil, I ran and directed my course aright.

Rouse Yourself, come to my help and see!

For You, O Lord God of hosts, the God of
Israel, draw near to punish all the nations;
spare none of those who work evil.

Each evening they come back, howling like
dogs and prowling about the city.

There they are, bellowing with their
mouths, and a sword is on their lips, for
they think, "Who has heard?"

But You, O Lord, will laugh them to
scorn; You will hold all the nations to be
nothing.

O my strength, I shall keep watch with you,
for You, O God, are my helper, and Your
mercy shall go before me.

My God will show me my enemies; slay
them not, lest they forget Your law.

Scatter them by Your power and bring them
down, O Lord, my defender!

For the sin of their mouths, the words of
their lips, let them be trapped in their
pride.

For the cursing and lies which they utter,
consume them in wrath;

consume them till they are no more, that
they may know that the God of Jacob
rules to the ends of the earth.

Each evening they come back, howling like
dogs and prowling about the city.

They roam about for food and growl if they
do not get their fill.

But I will sing of Your might; I will sing
aloud of Your mercy in the morning.

For You have been my defender and my
refuge in the day of my distress.

O My Helper, I will sing praises to You,
O my God, for You are my defender, the
God who shows me mercy.

PSALM 60 (59)

O God, You have rejected and destroyed
us; You have been angry; yet You showed
us mercy!

You have made the earth to quake, You
have troubled it; repair its breaches, for it
totters!

You have made Your people suffer hard
things; You have given us wine to drink
that made us reel.

You have set up a banner for those who fear
   You to rally to it from the bow.
That Your beloved may be delivered, save
   by Your right hand and hear me!
God has spoken in His sanctuary: "I will be
   exalted, and will divide up Shechem, and
   portion out the valley of Succoth.
Gilead is Mine and Manasseh is Mine;
   Ephraim is the protection of My head;
   Judah is My king.
Moab is My washbasin; upon Edom I will
   cast My shoe; the Philistines are subjected
   to Me."
Who will bring me to the fortified city?
   Who will lead me to Edom?
Will not You, O God, although You have
   rejected us? Will not You, O God, go
   forth with our armies?
Oh, grant us help in times of tribulation, for
   vain is the help of man!
With God we shall do valiantly; it is He
   who will bring our foes down to nothing.

Hear my cry, O Lord; listen to my prayer;

from the ends of the earth, I cried unto You
when my heart was troubled.

You lifted me up on a rock; You guided me,
for You were my hope, a strong tower
against the face of the enemy.

I will dwell in Your tabernacle forever; I
will shelter under the shadow of Your
wings!

For You, O God, have heard my prayers.

You have given an inheritance, O Lord, to
them that fear Your name.

You will prolong the life of the king; may
his years endure to all generations!

He will be enthroned forever before God.

Who will seek out His mercy and truth?

So will I ever sing praises to Your name,
that I may pay my vows day after day.

☩ ☩ ☩

PSALM 62 (61)

Shall not my soul be subjected to God? For
from Him comes my salvation.

He only is my God and my Savior, my
helper; I shall not be greatly moved.

How long will you set upon a man to shatter
him, all of you, like a leaning wall, a
tottering fence?

They plotted to thrust down my honor;
they take pleasure in falsehood.

They blessed with their mouths, but in their
hearts they cursed.

Nevertheless, O my soul, be subjected to
God, for from Him comes patience.

He only is my God and my Savior, my
helper; I shall not be moved.

On God rests my salvation and my glory,
the God of my help; my hope is in God.

Hope in Him, O assembly of the people;
pour out your heart before Him, for God
is our helper.

But the sons of men are vain, the sons of
men are a delusion; in the balances they
are false; they are all alike vanity.

Put no confidence in extortion; set no vain
hopes on robbery; if wealth increases, set
not your heart on it.

Once God has spoken; twice have I
heard this:

that power belongs to God, and that to You,
O Lord, belongs mercy.

For You requite everyone according to his
works.

PSALM 63 (62)

O God, You are my God; I seek You, my
soul thirsts for You;

my flesh faints for You, as in a dry and
weary land where no water is.

So I have looked upon You in the sanctuary,
beholding Your power and glory.

Because Your steadfast love is better than
life, my lips will praise You.

So I will bless You as long as I live; I will lift
up my hands and call on Your name.

My soul is feasted as with marrow and fat,
  and my mouth praises You with joyful lips

when I think of You upon my bed and
  meditate on You in the watches of the
  night.

For You have been my help, and in the
  shadow of Your wings I sing for joy.

My soul clings to You; Your right hand
  upholds me.

But those who seek to destroy my life shall
  go down into the depths of the earth;

they shall be given over to the power of the
  sword; they shall be prey for jackals.

But the king shall rejoice in God;

all who swear by Him shall glory; for the
  mouths of liars will be stopped.

PSALM 64 (63)

Hear my voice, O God, when I pray to You;
  deliver my soul from dread of the enemy.

You have hidden me from the secret plots of
  the wicked, from the crowd of evildoers,

who whet their tongues like swords, who
  have bent their bow with malice,

shooting from ambush at the blameless,
shooting at him suddenly and
without fear.

They have set up for themselves an evil
purpose; they talk of laying snares
secretly;

they have said, "Who will see them?" They
have sought out lawlessness.

They have wearied themselves with
searching cunningly.

A man shall come forth whose heart is deep,
and God will be exalted.

Their shafts became as children's arrows;
their words were of no effect and even
turned against them.

Then all men were in fear; they told what
God has wrought and understood what
He has done.

The righteous will rejoice in the Lord and
shall set his hope on Him.

Let all the upright in heart glory.

✠ ✠ ✠

KATHISMA 9—STASIS I

PSALM 65 (64)

Praise is due to You, O God, in Zion; and to
You shall vows be performed.

Hear my prayer; to You shall all flesh come.

The words of transgressors have led us
astray, but pardon our sins.

Blessed are those whom You have chosen
and taken to Yourself, O Lord; they shall
dwell in Your courts.

We shall be satisfied with the goodness
of Your house; holy is Your temple,
wonderful in righteousness.

Hear us, O God our Savior, the hope of all
the ends of the earth, and of those who
are far off beyond the sea;

for by Your strength You established the
mountains, being girded with might;

You trouble the depths of the seas, the
roaring of their waves.

The peoples shall be troubled, and those
who dwell at earth's farthest bounds will
be afraid at Your signs;

You will make the outgoings of the morning
and the evening to shout for joy.

You have visited the earth and watered it;
You greatly enrich it.

The river of God is full of water; You
provide their grain, for so You have
prepared it.

Water its furrows abundantly; multiply its
fruits; send forth gentle showers upon the
earth, that it may rejoice and bear fruit.

You will bless the seasons of the year with
Your goodness; Your fields shall be filled
with fatness.

The pastures of the desert will be lush and
green, and the hills shall gird themselves
with joy;

the meadows shall clothe themselves with
flocks, the valleys shall deck themselves
with grain;

they shall shout and sing together for joy!

Make a joyful noise to God, all the earth!
   Sing of His name; give glory to His praise!
Say to God, "How awesome are Your deeds!
   So great is Your power that Your enemies
   cringe before You."
Let all the earth worship You and
   praise You. Let it praise Your name,
   O Most High!
Come and see what God has done: He is
   terrible in His counsels among the sons
   of men.
He turns the sea into dry land; men will
   pass through the river on foot; there will
   we rejoice in Him.
He rules by His might forever; His eyes
   keep watch on the nations; let not those
   who provoke Him exalt themselves.
Bless our God, O peoples; make the sound
   of His praise be heard,
who keeps my soul among the living and
   does not let my feet slip.
For You, O God, have tested us; You have
   tried us with fire as silver is tried.

You brought us into the net; You laid
affliction on our backs; You let men ride
over our heads;

we went through fire and through water, yet
You have brought us forth to a place of
refreshment.

I will go into Your house with whole burnt
offerings;

I will pay You my vows, that which my lips
uttered and my mouth promised when I
was in trouble.

I will offer to You whole burnt offerings
full of marrow, with incense and rams; I
will make an offering to You of bulls and
goats.

Come and hear, all who fear God, and I will
tell what He has done for my soul.

I cried aloud to Him with my mouth, and
He was extolled with my tongue.

If I have cherished iniquity in my heart, let
the Lord not listen to me.

But truly God has listened; He has given
heed to the voice of my prayer.

Blessed be God, because He has not
rejected my prayer or removed His mercy
from me!

PSALM 67 (66)

O God, be bountiful to us and bless us!

Shine the light of Your countenance upon
us and have mercy on us,

that we may know Your way upon the earth
and Your salvation among all nations.

Let the peoples give thanks to You, O God;
let all the peoples give thanks to You!

Let the nations be glad and sing for joy, for
You judge the peoples with equity and
guide the nations upon the earth.

Let the peoples give thanks to You, O God;
let all the peoples give thanks to You!

The earth has yielded its fruit; let God, our
God, bless us.

Let God bless us, and let all the ends of the
earth fear Him!

✠ ✠ ✠

PSALM 68 (67)

Let God arise; let His enemies be scattered;
  let those who hate Him flee from before
  His Face!

As smoke vanishes, so let them vanish—as
  wax melts before the fire.

So the sinners will perish before the Face of
  God, but let the righteous be glad.

Let them exult before God; let them be
  jubilant with joy!

Sing to God, sing praises to His name;
  lift up a song to Him who rides upon
  the clouds; the Lord is His name, exult
  before Him!

They shall be troubled before the Face of
  Him who is Father of the fatherless and
  judge of the widows: so is God in His holy
  habitation.

God gives the desolate a home to dwell in;
  He leads out prisoners with strength, even
  the rebellious who dwell in the tombs.

O God, when You went forth before Your
people, when You marched through the
wilderness,

the earth quaked, yes, the heavens poured
down rain before the Face of the God of
Sinai, before the Face of the God of Israel.

O God, You will grant Your inheritance
a gracious rain; You restored it as it
languished;

Your flock found a dwelling in it; in Your
goodness, O God, You provide for
the poor.

The Lord God will give His Word to those
proclaiming the good news with great
power.

The king of the Beloved's armies will divide
the spoil for the beauty of the house.

Even if you stay among the sheepfolds, you
will have the wings of a dove covered
with silver, its breast with gleaming gold.

When the Most High places kings about
it, they will be made white as snow on
Zalmon.

The mountain of God is a fertile mountain,
a mountain rich like curdled milk—a rich
mountain.

Why do you look with envy at other rich
mountains?

This is the mountain God desired for His
abode, yes, where the Lord will dwell
until the end.

The chariots of God are ten thousand,
thousands of those who rejoice.

The Lord is among them on Sinai, in the
holy place.

You ascended on high, leading captivity
captive,

and gave gifts to men, even to the rebellious,
that You might dwell among them.

Blessed be the Lord God; blessed be the
Lord from day to day, and may the God of
our salvation prosper us,

for He is our God, the God of salvation;
and to God the Lord belongs escape from
death.

But God will shatter the heads of His
enemies, the hairy crown of those who
walk in their guilty ways.

The Lord said, "I will bring them back
from Bashan; I will bring them back from
the depths of the sea

that you may bathe your feet in blood, that
the tongues of your dogs may have their
portion from the foe."

We have seen Your processions, O God, the
processions of my God, the King, into the
sanctuary:

the princes in front of those who play
instruments, between the maidens playing
timbrels.

Bless God in the congregations; the Lord,
O you who are of Israel's fountain.

There is Benjamin, the younger of them, in
ecstasy; the princes of Judah, their rulers;
the princes of Zebulun, the princes of
Naphtali.

Summon Your might, O God; strengthen,
O God, what You have wrought for us.

Because of Your temple at Jerusalem, kings
will bear gifts to You.

Rebuke the beasts that dwell among the
reeds, the herd of bulls with the heifers of
the peoples,

lest they shut out those who have been
proved like silver: scatter the peoples who
delight in war.

Men of prayer shall come from Egypt;
Ethiopia shall hasten to stretch out her
hands readily to God.

Sing to God, O kingdoms of the earth; sing
psalms to the Lord.

Sing to God, who rides on the heaven of
heavens toward the east; lo, He sends
forth His resounding voice, a mighty
voice.

Ascribe glory to God! His majesty is over
Israel, and His power is in the clouds!

God is glorious in His saints, the God of
Israel!

He gives power and strength to His people;
blessed be God!

✠ ✠ ✠

PSALM 69 (68)

Save me, O God! For the waters have come up to my neck.

I am sunk in deep mire, where there is no foothold; I have come into the depths of the sea, and a storm sweeps over me.

I am weary with my crying; my throat has become hoarse; my eyes have grown dim with waiting for my God.

More in number than the hairs of my head are those who hated me without a cause;

my enemies who would persecute me unrighteously are strengthened; what I did not owe, they made me repay.

O God, You know my folly; the wrongs I have done are not hidden from You.

Let not those who hope on You be put to shame through me, O Lord God of hosts;

let not those who seek You be brought to dishonor through me, O God of Israel.

For it is for Your sake that I have borne reproach, that shame has covered my face.

I became a stranger to my brethren, a
foreigner to my mother's sons.

For zeal for Your house has consumed me,
and the insults of those who insulted You
have fallen on me.

When I humbled my soul with fasting, it
became my reproach.

When I made sackcloth my clothing, I
became a byword to them.

I am the talk of those who sit in the gate,
and the drunkards make songs about me.

But as for me, through my prayer I remain
close to You, O Lord; it is time to show
Your good will, O God.

In the abundance of Your mercy hear me, in
the truth of Your salvation.

Rescue me from sinking in the mire; let me
be delivered from those who hate me and
from the deep waters.

Let not the flood drown me, or the deep
swallow me up, or the pit close its mouth
over me.

Hear me, O Lord, for Your mercy is good;
according to the abundance of Your
compassion, look upon me.

Turn not away Your Face from Your servant, for I am afflicted.

Hear me speedily; attend to my soul and deliver it; deliver me because of my enemies!

For You know that I am reproached, covered with shame and dishonored; all who afflict me are before You.

My soul came to expect reproach and misery.

I looked for one to grieve with me, but there was none, and for one to comfort me, but I found none.

They gave me gall for food, and for my thirst they gave me vinegar to drink.

Let their table before them become a snare, a just retribution and a stumbling block.

Let their eyes be darkened so that they should not see, and bow down their backs continually.

Pour out Your wrath upon them, and let the fury of Your anger take hold of them.

May their habitation be a desolation; let no one dwell in their tents.

For they persecute him whom You have smitten, and they have added to the grief of my wounds.

Let them add iniquity to their iniquity, that they may have no access to Your justice.

Let them be blotted out of the book of the living; let them not be enrolled among the righteous.

But I am poor and afflicted; let Your salvation, O God, help me.

I will praise the name of my God with a song; I will magnify Him with praise.

This will please God more than a bull with horns and hooves.

The poor see and rejoice; seek the Lord, and your soul shall live.

For the Lord hears the poor and does not despise His own that are in bonds.

Let the heavens and the earth praise Him, the seas and all things that move in them.

For God will save Zion, and the cities of Judah will be rebuilt;

His servants shall dwell there and will inherit it;

the children of His servants shall possess it,
and those who love His name shall dwell
in it.

PSALM 70 (69)

Be pleased, O Lord, to deliver me; O Lord,
make haste to help me!

Let them be put to shame and confusion
who seek my life.

Let them be turned back and brought to
dishonor who desire my hurt.

Let them be appalled because of their shame
who say, "Aha! Aha!"

May all who seek You rejoice and be glad in
You! May those who love Your salvation
say evermore, "God is great!"

But I am poor and needy; hasten to me,
O God!

You are my help and deliverer; O Lord, do
not delay.

PSALM 71 (70)

In You, O Lord, have I hoped; let me never
be put to shame!

In Your righteousness, deliver me and
rescue me; incline Your ear to me and
save me!

Be a God of protection for me, a house of
refuge in order to save me; for You are my
fortress and my refuge.

Rescue me, O my God, from the hand of the
wicked, from the grasp of the transgressor
and unjust man.

For You, O Lord, are my support, my hope,
O Lord, from my youth.

Upon You I have leaned from birth; You are
my protector from my mother's womb.
My praise is continually of You.

I have become as a portent to many, but You
are my strong helper.

Let my mouth be filled with Your praise,
O Lord, that I may sing of Your glory and
honor all the day long.

Do not cast me off in the time of old age;
　forsake me not when my strength is spent.

For my enemies have spoken against me;
　those who watch for my soul consult
　together and say,

"God has forsaken him; pursue and lay hold
　of him, for there is none to deliver him."

O God, do not go far from me; O my God,
　come near to my help.

Let those who plot against my soul be put
　to shame and consumed; with scorn and
　disgrace may they be covered who seek
　my hurt.

But I will hope continually and will praise
　You yet more and more.

My mouth will tell openly of Your
　righteousness, of Your deeds of salvation
　all the day, for I am ignorant of the affairs
　of men.

I will go on in the might of the
　Lord; O Lord, I will speak of Your
　righteousness alone.

O God, from my youth You have taught me,
　and I still proclaim Your wonders even
　until I am old and advanced in years.

O God, do not forsake me till I proclaim
Your arm to all the generations to come,

Your power and Your righteousness, O God,
up to the highest heavens.

The mighty works You have done, O God!
Who is like You?

You have made me see many sore troubles!
Yet You turned and revived me and
brought me again from the depths of the
earth.

You increased Your greatness, and turned
and comforted me, and brought me again
from the depths of the earth.

Therefore I will also give thanks to You,
O God, because of Your truth, on an
instrument of psalmody;

I will sing praises to You with the harp, O
Holy One of Israel.

My lips will rejoice when I sing of You; my
soul also, which You have redeemed;

and my tongue will talk of Your righteous
help all the day long,

while those who sought to do me hurt are
put to shame and disgraced.

Give the king Your judgment, O God, and
  Your righteousness to the king's son,
that he may judge Your people with
  righteousness and Your poor with justice!
Let the mountains receive peace for the
  people and the hills, righteousness.
He shall uphold the right of the poor of His
  people.
Save the children of the needy and crush
  the false accuser!
And he shall continue as long as the sun and
  the moon, forever!
He shall come down as dew upon a fleece
  and as the rain which falls upon the earth.
In his days shall righteousness flourish and
  peace abound till the moon be no more.
He shall have dominion from sea to sea and
  from the river to the ends of the earth.
The Ethiopians will bow down before him,
  and his enemies lick the dust.
The kings of Tarshish and of the isles will
  bring presents; the kings of Sheba and
  Seba will offer gifts.

And all kings will worship him, all nations
serve him.

For he has delivered the poor from the
oppressor, and the needy who had no
helper.

He will spare the poor and needy and
deliver the souls of the needy.

From usury and injustice he will redeem
their souls, and his name will be in honor
before them.

And he will live, and gold of Arabia shall be
given to him.

And men will pray for him continually, and
all the day shall they praise him.

He will be a firm support on the earth and
on the tops of the mountains;

his fruit will be exalted higher than
Lebanon, and they will flourish in the
city like the grass of the field.

May his name be blessed forever! His name
shall endure longer than the sun!

All the tribes of the earth will be blessed in
him; all nations will call him blessed.

Blessed be the Lord, the God of Israel, who
alone does wondrous things.

Blessed be His glorious name forever; all the
earth will be filled with His glory!

Amen and Amen!

✠ ✠ ✠

KATHISMA 10—STASIS II

PSALM 73 (72)

How good is God to Israel, to the upright
in heart!

But my feet were almost overthrown; my
steps had almost slipped.

For I was envious of the transgressors when
I saw the tranquility of sinners.

For there is no torment at their time of
death; they remain firm in afflictions.

They are exempt from the troubles of men;
they are not scourged along with them.

Therefore pride has possessed them; they
have clothed themselves with their
injustice and ungodliness.

Their fatness drips with injustice; they
follow the desires of their hearts.

They have taken counsel and spoken in
wickedness; loftily they have uttered
unrighteousness.

They have set their mouths against heaven,
and their tongue struts through the earth.

Therefore my people turn to them, since
days of fullness are found with them.

And they say, "How can God know? Is there
knowledge in the Most High?"

Behold, these are the sinners, those who
always prosper; they have possessed
wealth.

And I said, "Have I in vain kept my
heart clean and washed my hands in
innocence?" For all the day long was I
stricken, and chastened every morning.

If I had said, "I will speak thus," I would
have broken covenant with the generation
of Your children.

So I thought how to understand this;

it was for me a wearisome task, until I went
into the sanctuary of God and I perceived
their end.

Truly, for their crafty dealings You set a
  judgment for them; You cast them down
  when they were lifted up.
How they have become desolate! Suddenly
  they have failed; they have perished
  because of their iniquity.
They are like a dream when one awakes;
  O Lord, You have wiped out their image
  from Your city.
My heart burned, and my reins were
  troubled; I was brutish and ignorant; I
  was like a beast before You.
Nevertheless I am continually with You;
  You have held my right hand.
You have guided me with Your counsel, and
  You have taken me to Yourself with glory.
For whom have I in heaven but You?
  And what have I desired upon earth
  besides You?
My flesh and my heart have failed, but
  God is the strength of my heart and my
  portion forever.
For lo, those who remove themselves far
  from You shall perish; You put an end to
  those who commit adultery against You.

But for me, my fullness is to cling to God,
to put my trust in the Lord God, that I
may proclaim Your praises in the gates of
the daughter of Zion!

PSALM 74 (73)

O God, why do You cast us off forever?
Why does Your anger smoke against the
sheep of Your pasture?
Remember Your congregation which You
have gotten of old!
You delivered the scepter of Your
inheritance, Mount Zion where You have
dwelt.
Continually lift up Your hands against their
pride, against all that the enemy has done
wickedly in Your sanctuary.
Those who hate You have boasted in the
midst of Your feast;
they have set up their own emblems on
the doorposts, in place of ours, without
knowing what they were doing.
As one fells trees in a forest with axes, they
have broken down its doors; they have
broken them down with axe and hammer.

They have burnt Your sanctuary to the ground; they desecrated the dwelling place of Your name.

They and all their acquaintances together have said in their hearts, "Come, let us abolish the feasts of the Lord from the face of the earth."

We do not see our emblems; there is no longer any prophet; and no one will recognize us anymore.

How long, O God, is the foe to scoff? Is the enemy to revile Your name forever?

Why do You turn back Your hand, Your right hand, from Your bosom forever?

Yet God is our King before the ages; He has worked salvation in the midst of the earth!

You established the sea by Your might; You broke the heads of the dragons in the waters.

You crushed the heads of the dragon; You gave him for food to the nations of Ethiopia.

You cut open springs and brooks; You dried up ever-flowing rivers.

Yours is the day, Yours also the night; You
have established the luminaries and
the sun.

You have fixed all the bounds of the earth;
You have made summer and winter.

Remember: The enemy has reproached the
Lord, and a foolish people reviles Your
name.

Do not deliver to the wild beasts a soul that
gives praise to You; do not forget the life
of Your poor forever.

Look upon Your covenant, for the
dark places of the land are full of the
habitations of violence.

Let not the afflicted and shamed be rejected;
the poor and needy shall praise Your
name.

Arise, O God, plead Your cause; remember
the insults uttered against You by the fool
all the day long.

Do not forget the cry of Your supplicants,
for the pride of those who hate You goes
up continually!

PSALM 75 (74)

We will give thanks to You, O God; we
give thanks and call on Your name; I will
recount Your wondrous deeds.

"At the set time which I appoint, I will
judge with equity.

The earth is dissolved, and all its
inhabitants. I keep steady its pillars."

I say to the transgressors, "Do not
transgress," and to the sinners, "Do not
lift up your horn.

Do not lift up your horn on high or speak
unrighteousness against God,

for salvation comes not from the east or
from the west, and not from the desert
mountains."

For God is the judge, putting down one and
lifting up another.

For in the hand of the Lord there is a cup
with unmixed wine, blended with spices,
and He has poured it from cup to cup,

but its dregs have not been totally poured
out; all the sinners of the earth shall
drink them.

But I will rejoice forever; I will sing praises
to the God of Jacob.

All the horns of the wicked I will cut off,
but the horn of the righteous shall be
exalted.

PSALM 76 (75)

In Judah God is known; His name is great
in Israel.

His abode has been in Salem and His
dwelling place in Zion.

There He broke the power of the bow, the
shield, the sword, and the battle.

You shine forth wondrously from the
everlasting mountains.

All those whose hearts are without
understanding were troubled; they slept
their sleep and found nothing left in their
hands—those who were greedy for wealth.

At Your rebuke, O God of Jacob, the riders
on the horses slumbered.

But You are terrible! Who can stand before You? Your anger has been known from of old.

You caused judgment to be heard from heaven; the earth feared and was still

when God arose to establish judgment, to save all the meek in heart.

Therefore, the inward thought of man shall confess You, and the remembrance of it shall be as a feast.

Pray and make Your vows before the Lord our God; all who are around Him shall bring gifts to Him who is to be feared,

who cuts off the spirit of princes, who is terrible to the kings of the earth!

PSALM 77 (76)

I cried aloud to God with my voice; my voice cried aloud to God, and He heard me.

In the day of my trouble, I earnestly sought the Lord; in the night my hands were stretched out before Him, and I was not deceived; my soul refused any other consolation.

I remembered God, and I rejoiced; when I thought of my woes, my spirit failed.

My eyes were awake in vigil; I was so troubled that I could not speak.

I considered the days of old; I remembered the eternal years, and I meditated.

I labored in my heart in the night, and my spirit struggled to understand:

Will the Lord spurn forever and never again be favorable?

Has He cut off His mercy forever, from generation to generation?

Will God forget to be gracious? Will He in anger shut up His compassion?

And I said, "Now have I begun; this is the change of the right hand of the Most High."

I called to mind the deeds of the Lord; yes, I will remember Your wonders from the beginning.

I will meditate on all Your works and muse on Your deeds.

Your way, O God, is in holiness: Who is so great a God as our God?

You are the God who works wonders; You have manifested Your might among the peoples.

With Your arm You redeemed Your people, the sons of Jacob and Joseph.

The waters saw You, O God; the waters saw You and were afraid; yes, the deeps trembled.

There was a great sound of waters; the clouds gave forth voice; Your arrows went abroad.

The crash of Your thunder was in the whirlwind; Your lightning lighted up the world; the earth trembled and shook.

Your way is through the sea, Your paths through many waters; yet Your footprints are unknown.

You led Your people like sheep by the hand of Moses and Aaron.

✠ ✠ ✠

KATHISMA 11—STASIS I

PSALM 78 (77)

Give ear, O my people, to my law; incline
  your ears to the words of my mouth!
I will open my mouth in parables; I will
  utter dark sayings from of old,
things that we have heard and known, that
  our fathers have told us.
They did not hide them from their children
  so that they would tell them to the
  coming generation;
that they would declare the praises of
  the Lord and His mighty acts, and the
  wonders which He has wrought.
He established a testimony in Jacob and
  appointed a law in Israel,
which He commanded our fathers to make
  known to their children,
that the next generation might know them,
  the children yet unborn,
and arise and tell them to their children, so
  that they should set their hope in God

and not forget the works of God but observe
His commandments;

that they should not be like their fathers, a
stubborn and rebellious generation,

a generation whose heart was not steadfast,
whose spirit was not faithful to God.

The sons of Ephraim, bending and shooting
the bow, turned back on the day of battle.

They did not keep God's covenant and
would not walk according to His law.

And they forgot His benefits and His
miracles He had shown them,

the miracles He wrought in the sight of
their fathers, in the land of Egypt, in the
fields of Tanis.

He divided the sea and led them through it,
and made the waters stand as in a bottle.

In the daytime He led them with a cloud,
and all the night with a fiery light.

He cleft rocks in the wilderness and gave
them drink abundantly as from the deep.

He made streams come out of the rock and
caused waters to flow down like rivers.

Yet they sinned still more against Him,
provoking the Most High in the desert.

They tested God in their heart by
　　demanding the food they craved in
　　their soul.
They also spoke against God, saying, "Can
　　God spread a table in the wilderness?
He smote the rock so that water gushed out
　　and streams overflowed.
Can He also give bread or prepare a table
　　for His people?"
Therefore the Lord heard and was full of
　　wrath; a fire was kindled against Jacob;
　　His anger mounted against Israel,
because they had no faith in God and did
　　not trust in His salvation.
Yet He commanded the clouds from above
　　and opened the doors of heaven,
and He rained down upon them manna to
　　eat and gave them the bread of heaven.
Man ate of the bread of the angels; He sent
　　them food in abundance.
He raised the east wind from heaven, and
　　by His power He led out the south wind;
He rained flesh upon them like dust,
　　winged birds like the sand of the seas;

they fell in the midst of their camp, all
around their tents.

And they ate and were well filled, for He
gave them what they craved.

They were not disappointed in their desire,
yet while the food was still in their
mouths, the anger of God rose against
them,

and He slew the strongest of them and laid
low the picked men of Israel.

In spite of all this, they still sinned; they did
not believe in His wonders.

And their days were consumed in vanity
and their years in anxiety.

When He slew them, they sought for Him;
they returned and sought God earnestly.

They remembered that God was their
helper, the Most High God their
Redeemer.

But they flattered Him with their mouths;
they lied to Him with their tongues.

Their heart was not true toward Him; they
were not steadfast in His covenant.

Yet He is compassionate and will forgive
their sins, and will not destroy them;

yes, He will restrain His anger often and
will not stir up all His wrath.

He remembered that they are but flesh, a
wind that passes and comes not again.

How often they provoked Him in the
wilderness and angered Him in the
desert!

Yes, they turned back and tested God and
provoked the Holy One of Israel.

They did not keep in mind His hand, the
day when He redeemed them from the
hand of the oppressor;

when He had wrought His signs in Egypt
and His miracles in the fields of Tanis,
and had turned their rivers to blood, and
their streams so that they could not drink.

He sent among them swarms of flies,
which devoured them, and frogs, which
destroyed them.

He gave their crops to the canker worm and
their labors to the locust.

He destroyed their vines with hail and their
sycamores with frost.

He gave over their cattle to the hail and
their possessions to fire.

He let loose on them the fierceness of His
anger, wrath, indignation, and distress, a
company of destroying angels.

He made a path for His anger; He did not
spare their souls from death, but gave
even their cattle over to death.

He smote every firstborn in the land of
Egypt, the first fruits of their labors in
the tents of Ham.

And He led out His people like sheep and
guided them in the wilderness like a
flock.

And He guided them with hope, so that
they were not afraid; but the sea covered
their enemies.

And He brought them to the mountain of
His holiness, this mountain which His
right hand had won.

He drove out nations before them; He
apportioned for them an inheritance by
line and settled the tribes of Israel in
their tents.

Yet they tested and provoked the Most High
God and did not observe His testimonies.

And they turned away and broke covenant
like their fathers; they became like a
twisted bow.

And they provoked Him to wrath with their
high places; they moved Him to jealousy
with their graven images.

God heard and despised them, and He
utterly rejected Israel.

He rejected the tabernacle at Shiloh, His
tent where He dwelt among men,

and delivered their power into captivity,
their beauty to the hand of the foe.

He gave His people over to the sword and
despised His heritage.

Fire devoured their young men, and their
maidens were not mourned.

Their priests fell by the sword, and their
widows were not lamented.

Then the Lord awoke as one from sleep,
like a strong man excited by wine.

And He smote His adversaries as they fled;
He put them to everlasting shame.

And He rejected the tabernacle of Joseph;
He did not choose the tribe of Ephraim;

but He chose the tribe of Judah, Mount
   Zion which He loved: He fashioned it for
   His holy abode, like the earth, which He
   has founded forever.
He chose David His servant and took him
   up from the flocks of sheep;
He took him from following the ewes with
   young to be the shepherd of Jacob His
   servant and Israel His inheritance.
And he tended them in the innocence
   of his heart and guided them with the
   skillfulness of his hands.

✠ ✠ ✠

KATHISMA 11—STASIS II

PSALM 79 (78)

O God, the nations have come into Your
   inheritance;
they have defiled Your holy temple; they
   have made Jerusalem a storage place for
   crops.

They have given the dead bodies of Your
servants to the birds of the air for food,
the flesh of Your saints to the beasts of the
earth.

They have poured out their blood like water
round about Jerusalem, and there was
none to bury them.

We have become a taunt to our neighbors,
mockery and derision to those round
about us.

How long, O Lord? Will You be angry
forever? Will Your jealous wrath burn
like fire?

Pour out Your anger on the nations that
have not known You and on the kingdoms
that have not called on Your name!

For they have devoured Jacob and laid waste
his habitation.

Do not remember our transgressions from
of old;

let Your tender mercies, O Lord, speedily
go before us, for we have become
exceedingly poor.

Help us, O God of our salvation, for the
glory of Your name.

O Lord, deliver us and purge away our sins
for Your name's sake, lest by chance the
nations say, "Where is their God?"
Let the avenging of the outpoured blood
of Your servants be known among the
nations before our eyes!
Let the groans of the captives come before
You; according to Your great power,
preserve the sons of those who were slain!
Return sevenfold into the bosom of our
neighbors the taunts with which they
have taunted You, O Lord!
Then we, Your people, the sheep of Your
pasture, will give thanks to You forever;
throughout all generations, we will recount
Your praise.

PSALM 80 (79)

Give ear, O Shepherd of Israel, You who
lead Joseph like a flock; manifest Yourself,
You who sit upon the cherubim.
O Lord, raise up Your might before
Ephraim and Benjamin and Manasseh,
and come to save us!

Lead us back, O Lord; let Your Face shine, and we will be saved.

O Lord God of hosts, how long will You be angry with the prayer of Your servant?

How long will You feed us with the bread of tears and cause us to drink tears in full measure?

You have made us an object of contention to our neighbors, and our enemies have mocked us.

Lead us back, O Lord God of hosts; let Your Face shine, and we will be saved.

You brought a vine out of Egypt; You drove out the nations and planted it.

You made a way for it and planted its roots, and it filled the land.

Its shadow covered the mountains, its branches the cedars of God.

It sent out its branches to the sea and its shoots to the river.

Why then have You broken down its hedge so that all who pass along the way pluck its fruit?

The boar from the forest ravages it, and the wild beast has devoured it.

Return, O God of hosts, we pray; look
down from heaven and see and visit
this vine.

Restore what Your right hand has planted
and look on the son of man, whom You
have made strong for Yourself.

It is burnt with fire and dug up; they will
perish at the rebuke of Your countenance!

Let Your hand be upon the man of Your
right hand, on the son of man whom You
have made strong for Yourself.

Then we will never turn back from You;
You will give us life, and we will call on
Your name.

Lead us back, O Lord God of hosts; let Your
Face shine, and we will be saved.

PSALM 81 (80)

Rejoice in God our helper; rejoice greatly
in the Living God!

Take up a psalm and sound the timbrel, the
sweet psaltery with the harp.

Blow the trumpet at the new moon on this
solemn day of our feast.

For it is a statute for Israel, an ordinance of
the God of Jacob.

He made it a testimony in Joseph when he
went out from the land of Egypt;

he heard a language he did not understand.

He relieved his back from forced labors, for
his hands slaved in making baskets.

"In distress you called on Me, and I
delivered you;

I heard you in the secret place of the storm;
I tested you at the waters of rebellion.

Hear, O my people, and I will speak to you,
O Israel; I will testify to you:

If you listen to me, there shall be no new
god among you;

you shall not worship a foreign god.

For I am the Lord your God, who brought
you up out of the land of Egypt.

Open your mouth wide, and I will fill it.

But my people did not listen to My voice;
Israel gave no heed to Me.

So I let them follow their own hearts; they
shall go on in their own ways.

If My people had listened to Me, if Israel
had walked in My ways,

I would very soon have subdued their
enemies and made their oppressors feel
the weight of My hand."

The enemies of the Lord tried to deceive
Him; the time of their punishment shall
be forever.

But He fed his own with the finest of the
wheat and satisfied them with honey from
the rock.

✠ ✠ ✠

KATHISMA 11—STASIS III

PSALM 82 (81)

God stands in the divine assembly; in their
midst, He judges the gods!

How long will you judge unjustly and take
the side of sinners?

Give justice to the orphan and the destitute;
uphold the right of the lowly and
the poor.

Rescue the poor and destitute, and deliver
him out of the hand of the sinner.

They have neither knowledge nor
understanding: they walk about in
darkness; all the foundations of the earth
shall be shaken!

I have said, "You are gods, all of you sons of
the Most High;

but you shall die like all men and fall like
any prince."

Arise, O God, judge the earth: for to You
belong all the nations!

PSALM 83 (82)

O God, who is like unto You? Do not be
silent or be still, O God!

For lo, Your enemies make themselves
heard; those who hate You have raised
their head.

They have plotted wickedly against Your
people; they have conspired against Your
holy ones.

They have said, "Come, let us wipe them
out from the nations; let the name of
Israel be remembered no more!"

Yes, they conspire with one accord; against
You they make a covenant:

the tents of Edom and the Ishmaelites,
    Moab and the Hagrites,
Gebal and Ammon and Amalek, Philistia
    with the inhabitants of Tyre;
Assyria also has joined them; they have
    become a help to the children of Lot.
Do to them as You did to Midian and to
    Sisera, as to Jabin at the river Kishon,
who were utterly destroyed at Endor, who
    became dung for the ground.
Make their princes like Oreb and Zeeb, all
    the princes like Zebah and Zalmunna,
who said, "Let us take to ourselves the altar
    of God as an inheritance."
O my God, make them like whirling dust,
    like chaff before the wind.
As fire shall burn the forest, as the flame
    may consume the mountains,
so shall You pursue them with Your tempest
    and terrify them with Your anger!
Fill their faces with shame so that they shall
    seek Your name, O Lord.
Let them be put to shame and dismayed
    forever; yes, let them perish in disgrace.

Let the nations understand that Your name
is the Lord, that You alone are the Most
High over all the earth.

PSALM 84 (83)

How lovely are Your dwelling places,
O Lord of hosts!
My soul longs and faints for the courts of
the Lord; my heart and flesh sing for joy
to the living God.
Even the sparrow finds a home and the
swallow a nest for herself where she may
lay her young:
at Your altars, O Lord of hosts, my King
and my God.
Blessed are those who dwell in Your house,
ever singing Your praise!
Blessed are they whose strength is in You, in
whose heart are the highways to Zion.
They shall pass through the valley of tears
to the place which You appointed;
there the Lawgiver shall give blessings.
They will go from strength to strength; the
God of gods will be seen in Zion.

O Lord God of hosts, hear my prayer; give
ear, O God of Jacob!

Behold, O God our protector; look upon the
face of Your Anointed!

For a day in Your courts is better than a
thousand elsewhere.

I would rather be a doorkeeper in the house
of my God than dwell in the tents of
wickedness.

For the Lord God loves mercy and truth;
He bestows grace and glory.

No good thing does the Lord withhold
from those who walk uprightly.

O Lord of hosts, blessed is the man who
trusts in You!

PSALM 85 (84)

You have shown favor to Your land, O
Lord; You have brought back the captives
of Jacob.

You forgave the iniquity of Your people;
You pardoned all their sin.

You withdrew all Your wrath; You turned
from Your hot anger.

Restore us again, O God of our salvation,
and put away Your indignation toward us!

Will You be angry with us forever?
Will You prolong Your anger to all
generations?

O God, You will return and give us life, and
Your people will rejoice in You.

Show us Your mercy, O Lord, and grant us
Your salvation.

Let me hear what God the Lord will speak,
for He will speak peace to His people, to
His saints, to those who turn to Him in
their hearts.

Surely His salvation is at hand for those
who fear Him, that glory may dwell in
our land.

Mercy and truth have met; righteousness
and peace have kissed each other.

Truth arose from the earth, and
righteousness looked down from the sky.

Yes, the Lord will pour out His sweet
goodness, and our land will yield its fruit.

Righteousness will go before Him, and its
footsteps shall open the way.

PSALM 86 (85)

Incline Your ear, O Lord, and answer me,
   for I am poor and needy.

Preserve my life, for I am godly; save Your
   servant who trusts in You.

You are my God; be gracious to me, O Lord,
   for to You do I cry all the day.

Gladden the soul of Your servant, for to
   You, O Lord, do I lift up my soul.

For You, O Lord, are good and forgiving,
   abounding in mercy to all who call
   on You.

Give ear, O Lord, to my prayer; hearken to
   my cry of supplication.

In the day of my trouble I call on You, for
   You answer me.

There is none like You among the gods, O
   Lord, nor are there any works like Yours.

All the nations You have made shall come
   and bow down before You, O Lord, and
   shall glorify Your Name.

For You are great and do wondrous things;
You alone are God.

Lead me in Your way, O Lord, that I may
walk in Your truth; let my heart find its
joy in the fear of Your Name.

I give thanks to You, O Lord my God, with
my whole heart, and I will glorify Your
Name forever.

For great is Your mercy toward me; You
have delivered my soul from the depths of
Sheol.

O God, insolent men have risen up against
me; a band of ruthless men seek my life,
and they do not set You before them.

But You, O Lord, are a God compassionate
and merciful, longsuffering, and
abounding in mercy and truth.

Look upon me and take pity on me; give
Your strength to Your servant and save
the son of Your handmaid.

Set upon me a sign of salvation, that those
who hate me may see and be put to shame,
because You, O Lord, have helped me and
comforted me.

His foundations rest upon the holy
mountains.

The Lord loves the gates of Zion more than
all the tabernacles of Jacob.

Glorious things have been spoken of you,
O City of God.

To those who know me, I will mention
Rahab and Babylon;

behold also the foreigners, and Tyre, with
the people of Ethiopia: all these were
born there.

"Zion is my mother," a man will say, for
such a man was born in her; and the Most
High Himself has established her.

The Lord shall record in the Scriptures of
the people and princes all those who were
born in her.

All those whose dwelling is within you
rejoice!

PSALM 88 (87)

O Lord, my God, I call for help by day; I
cry out in the night before You.

Let my prayer come before You; incline
Your ear to my cry!
For my soul is full of troubles, and my life
draws near to Sheol.
I am reckoned among those who go down to
the Pit; I am a man who has no strength,
like one forsaken among the dead, like the
slain that lie in the grave,
like those whom You remember no more,
for they are cut off from Your hand.
You have put me in the depths of the Pit, in
the regions dark and deep.
Your wrath lies heavy upon me, and You
overwhelm me with all Your waves.
You have caused my companions to shun
me; You have made me a thing of horror
to them.
I am shut in so that I cannot escape; my eyes
grow dim through sorrow.
Every day I call upon You, O Lord; I spread
out my hands to You.
Do You work wonders for the dead? Do the
shades rise up to praise You?
Is Your steadfast love declared in the grave
or Your faithfulness in Abaddon?

Are Your wonders known in the darkness
or Your saving help in the land of
forgetfulness?

But I, O Lord, cry to You; in the morning
my prayer comes before You.

O Lord, why do You cast me off? Why do
You hide Your Face from me?

Afflicted and close to death from my youth
up, I suffer Your terrors; I am helpless.

Your wrath has swept over me; Your dread
assaults destroy me.

They surround me like a flood all day long;
they close in upon me together.

You have caused lover and friend to shun
me; my companions are in darkness.

✠ ✠ ✠

KATHISMA 12—STASIS II

PSALM 89 (88)

I will sing of Your mercy, O Lord, forever;
with my mouth I will proclaim Your truth
to all generations.

For You have said, "Mercy will be established forever, and My truth will be prepared in the heavens.

I made a covenant with My chosen ones; I swore to David my servant,

'I will establish your seed forever and build up your throne to all generations.'"

The heavens praise Your wonders, O Lord, Your truth in the assembly of the saints!

For who in the skies can be compared to the Lord?

Who shall be likened to the Lord among the sons of God?

God is glorified in the council of the saints, great and terrible toward all that are round about Him.

O Lord God of hosts, who is like You?

You are mighty, O Lord, and Your truth is round about You.

You rule the might of the sea; You still the tumult of its waves.

You have humbled the proud, You have wounded him unto death,

and by the power of Your arm You have scattered Your enemies.

The heavens are Yours; the earth also is Yours; You have founded the world and its fullness.

The north and the west, You have created them; Tabor and Hermon shall rejoice in Your name!

Yours is the mighty arm; let Your hand be strengthened; let Your right hand be exalted.

Righteousness and judgment are the foundation of Your throne; mercy and truth shall go before Your Face.

Blessed are the people who know the festal shout!

O Lord, they shall walk in the light of Your countenance and shall exult in Your name forever and be exalted in Your righteousness.

For You are the boast of their strength, and in Your good pleasure our horn shall be exalted.

For our help is from the Lord and from the Holy One of Israel, our King.

Of old, You spoke in a vision to Your sons and said,

"I have laid help on one who is mighty; I
	have exalted one chosen from My people.
I have found David, My servant; with My
	holy oil I have anointed him;
for My hand shall support him, My arm
	shall strengthen him.
The enemy shall have no advantage against
	him, and the son of iniquity shall not
	hurt him.
And I will hew down his foes before him
	and put to flight those who hate him.
But My truth and My mercy shall be with
	him, and in My name shall his horn be
	exalted.
And I will set his hand on the sea and his
	right hand on the rivers.
He shall cry to me, 'You are my Father, my
	God, and the helper of my salvation.'
And I will make him the firstborn, higher
	than the kings of the earth.
My steadfast love I will keep for him
	forever, and My covenant will be firm
	for him.
And I will establish his seed forever and
	ever and his throne as the days of heaven.

If his sons forsake My law and do not walk
in My judgments,
if they violate My statutes and do not keep
My commandments,
then I will punish their transgressions with
a rod and their sins with scourges;
but I will not turn away from him My
mercy, nor in My truth will I bring
him harm.
I will by no means violate My covenant or
negate the word that went forth from
My lips.
Once for all I have sworn by My holiness
that I will not lie to David.
His seed shall endure forever and his throne
as the sun before Me, like the moon that
is established forever: faithful witnesses
in heaven."
Yet You have cast off and despised, You have
rejected Your anointed.
You have overthrown the covenant of Your
servant; You have defiled his sanctuary to
the ground.
You have broken down all his hedges; You
have filled his strongholds with terror.

All that pass by despoil him; he has become
a reproach to his neighbors.

You have exalted the right hand of his foes;
You have made all his enemies rejoice.

You have deprived him of the help of his
sword and have not supported him in
battle.

You have stripped him of his purity and cast
his throne to the ground.

You have cut short his days; You have
covered him with shame.

How long, O Lord, will You turn away?
Forever? Will Your wrath burn like fire?

Remember what my being is. Is it for
nothing that You have created all the sons
of men?

What man shall live and not see death, and
deliver his soul from the hand of Sheol?

O Lord, where are Your mercies of old,
which in Your truth You swore to David?

Remember, O Lord, the offenses which
many nations have committed against
Your servants and which I bear in my
bosom;

with which Your enemies taunt, O Lord,
with which they mock the advent of Your
anointed.

Blessed be the Lord forever! Amen and
Amen.

☩ ☩ ☩

KATHISMA 12—STASIS III

PSALM 90 (89)

Lord, You have been our refuge from
generation to generation.

Before the mountains were born and before
the earth and the world were formed, You
are from everlasting.

Do not turn men back to the dust and say,
"Turn back, O you sons of men."

For a thousand years in Your sight are but as
yesterday when it is past or as a watch in
the night.

What are the years of a man? In one
morning they pass away like grass:

in the morning it flourishes and thrives; in the evening it fades and withers.

For we are consumed by Your anger; by Your wrath we are overwhelmed.

You have set our iniquities before You, our deeds in the light of Your countenance.

Therefore, all our days are gone, and we have passed away under Your wrath; our years are like a spider's web.

The years of our life are threescore and ten, or even by reason of strength fourscore, and the greater part of them is toil and trouble;

but Your kindness comes upon us, and we are thus instructed.

Who considers the power of Your anger and measures the vehemence of Your wrath?

Manifest Your right hand that we may be instructed in our hearts with wisdom.

Return, O Lord! How long? Have pity on Your servants.

Satisfy us in the morning with Your steadfast love, that we may rejoice and be glad all our days.

Make us glad as many days as You have
    afflicted us and as many years as we have
    seen evil.
Let Your work be manifest to Your servants
    and Your glorious power to their children.
Let the favor of the Lord our God be upon
    us and establish the work of our hands.
Yes, establish the work of our hands.

PSALM 91 (90)

He who dwells in the shelter of the Most
    High will abide in the shadow of the
    Heavenly God.
He will say to the Lord, "My protector and
    my refuge, my God, in whom I trust."
For He will deliver you from the snare of
    the fowler and from the deadly pestilence;
He will cover you with His pinions, and
    under His wings you will find refuge;
His truth is a shield and buckler.
You will not fear the terror of the night, nor
    the arrow that flies by day,
nor the pestilence that stalks in darkness,
    nor the demon at noonday.

A thousand may fall at your side, ten
thousand at your right hand, but it will
not come near you.

You will only look with your eyes and see
the recompense of the wicked.

Because you have made the Lord your
refuge, the Most High your habitation,

no evil shall befall you, no scourge come
near your tent.

For He will give His angels charge of you, to
guard you in all your ways.

On their hands they will bear you up, lest
you dash your foot against a stone.

You will tread on the asp and the basilisk;
the lion and the dragon you will trample
underfoot.

"Because he cleaves to Me in love, I will
deliver him; I will protect him, because
he knows My name.

When he calls to Me, I will answer him; I
will be with him in trouble; I will rescue
him and glorify him.

With long life I will satisfy him and show
him My salvation."

Thursday—Matins (a)

KATHISMA 13—STASIS I

PSALM 92 (91)

It is good to give thanks to the Lord, to sing praises to Your name, O Most High!

To declare Your mercy in the morning and Your truth by night,

to the music of the lute and the harp, to the melody of the lyre.

For You, O Lord, have made me glad by Your work; at the works of Your hands I sing for joy.

How great are Your works, O Lord! Your thoughts are very deep!

A dull man cannot know, a fool cannot understand this.

Though the wicked sprout like grass and all evildoers flourish, they are doomed to destruction forever.

But You, O Lord, are Most High forever.

For lo, Your enemies, O Lord, for lo, Your enemies shall perish; all evildoers shall be scattered.

But my horn shall be exalted like the horn of the wild bull; my old age shall be strengthened by Your anointing.

My eyes have seen the downfall of my enemies, and my ears have heard the doom of my evil assailants.

The righteous flourish like the palm tree and grow like a cedar in Lebanon.

They are planted in the house of the Lord; they flourish in the courts of our God.

Their old age shall be fruitful, and they shall be ever full of vigor,

to declare that the Lord our God is righteous, and there is no unrighteousness in Him.

PSALM 93 (92)

The Lord is King; He is robed in majesty. The Lord is robed; He is girded with strength.

For He has established the world so that it shall never be moved.

Your throne is prepared from of old; You are from everlasting.

The rivers have lifted up, O Lord, the rivers
have lifted up their voice;

the rivers lift up their waves at the roaring
of many waters.

Mighty are the waves of the sea; the Lord
on high is mighty.

Your testimonies are very sure; holiness
befits Your house, O Lord, forevermore!

PSALM 94 (93)

The Lord is a God of vengeance; the God
of vengeance will act with boldness.

Arise, O Judge of the earth: render a reward
to the proud!

How long shall sinners, O Lord, how long
shall sinners boast?

How long will they utter and speak
unrighteousness; how long will all the
workers of iniquity lift up their voice?

They have afflicted Your people, O Lord,
and oppressed Your heritage.

They have slain the widow and the orphan
and murdered the foreigner.

And they said, "The Lord will not see; the
God of Jacob will not perceive."

Understand now; O you simple among the
people and fools, finally be wise.

He who planted the ear, does He not hear?
Or He who formed the eye, does He
not see?

He who admonishes the nations, shall
He not chastise—He who teaches man
knowledge?

The Lord knows the thoughts of men, that
they are vain.

Blessed is the man whom You will instruct,
O Lord, and will teach out of Your law,

to give him respite from evil days until a pit
is dug for the wicked.

For the Lord will not forsake His people;
He will not abandon His inheritance

until judgment again becomes righteous and
all the upright in heart follow it.

Who will rise up for me against the
transgressors?

Or who will stand up for me against the
workers of iniquity?

If the Lord had not helped me, my soul
would already have dwelt in Sheol.

When I said, "My foot slips," Your mercy,
O Lord, came to my help.

O Lord, in the same measure as the grief
within my heart, Your consolations filled
my soul with joy.

Shall the throne of the wicked have
fellowship with You, the throne which
makes mischief a statute?

They will hunt for the soul of the righteous
and condemn innocent blood.

But the Lord was my refuge, and my God
the foundation of my hope.

And He will bring back on them their
iniquity and their wickedness: the Lord
our God will wipe them out.

☩ ☩ ☩

KATHISMA 13—STASIS II

PSALM 95 (94)

Come, let us rejoice in the Lord! Let us
make a joyful noise to God our Savior!

Let us come before His Face with
thanksgiving; let us make a joyful noise to
Him with psalms!

For the Lord is a great God and a great King
over all the earth.

For in His hands are the depths of the earth;
the heights of the mountains are His also.

For the sea is His, for He made it; for His
hands formed the dry land.

Come, let us worship and fall down before
Him and weep before the Lord our
Maker!

For He is our God, and we are the people of
His pasture and the sheep of His hand.

Today, if you will hear His voice, harden
not your hearts, as in the rebellion, in the
day of trial in the wilderness,

where your fathers tested Me, tried Me, and
saw My works forty years.

Therefore I was angry with that generation
and said, "They always go astray in
their hearts, and they have not known
my ways."

So I swore in my wrath, "They shall not
enter My rest."

Sing to the Lord a new song; sing to the
Lord, all the earth!

Sing to the Lord, bless His name; from day
to day, proclaim the salvation of our God.

Declare His glory among the nations, His
marvelous works among all peoples!

For great is the Lord and greatly to be
praised; He is terrible above all gods.

For all the gods of the peoples are idols; but
the Lord made the heavens.

Praise and beauty are before Him; holiness
and majesty are in His sanctuary.

Bring to the Lord, O families of the
peoples, bring to the Lord glory and
honor!

Bring to the Lord the glory due His name;
bring offerings and come into His courts!

Worship the Lord in His holy court; let all
the earth tremble before Him!

Say among the nations that the Lord
is King!

For He has established the world so that it
shall never be moved; He will judge the
peoples with equity.

Let the heavens be glad, and let the earth
  rejoice; let the sea be moved, and all that
  fills it!
The field shall exult, and everything in it;
  then shall all the trees of the wood rejoice
  before the Face of the Lord;
for He comes, for He comes to judge the
  earth.
He will judge the world with righteousness
  and the peoples with His truth.

PSALM 97 (96)

The Lord reigns; let the earth rejoice; let
  the many coastlands be glad!
Clouds and darkness are round about
  Him; righteousness and justice are the
  foundation of His throne.
Fire shall go before Him and burn up His
  adversaries round about.
His lightnings appeared to the world; the
  earth saw and trembled.
The mountains melted like wax before the
  Face of the Lord, before the Face of the
  Lord of all the earth.

The heavens have proclaimed His
righteousness, and all the people have
beheld His glory.

Let all worshipers of images be put to shame
who make their boast in their idols.

Bow down before Him, all His angels!

Zion heard and was glad, and the daughters
of Judah rejoiced because of Your
judgments, O Lord.

For You are Lord Most High over all the
earth; You are exalted far above all gods.

You that love the Lord, hate evil; the Lord
preserves the souls of His saints; He shall
deliver them from the hand of sinners.

Light dawns for the righteous and joy for
the upright in heart!

Rejoice in the Lord, O you righteous, and
confess the holiness of His name!

✠ ✠ ✠

PSALM 98 (97)

Sing to the Lord a new song, for the Lord has done marvelous things!

His right hand and His holy arm have wrought salvation for Him.

The Lord has made known His salvation; He has revealed His righteousness before the nations.

He has remembered His mercy to Jacob and His truth to the house of Israel.

All the ends of the earth have seen the salvation of our God!

Shout to God, all the earth; sing and exult and sing psalms!

Sing to the Lord with a lyre, with a lyre and the voice of a psalm!

With trumpets of metal and the sound of a trumpet of horn, make a joyful noise to the Lord before the king.

Let the sea be shaken and all its fullness, the world and those who dwell in it!

The rivers will clap their hands; the mountains will exult.

For He has come to judge the earth; He will judge the world in righteousness and the peoples with equity.

PSALM 99 (98)

The Lord reigns; let the peoples tremble! He sits enthroned upon the cherubim; let the earth quake!

The Lord is great in Zion; He is exalted over all the peoples.

Let them confess the greatness of Your name, for it is terrible and holy, and the king's honor is to love justice.

You have prepared equity; You have executed judgment and justice in Jacob.

Extol the Lord our God; worship at His footstool, for He is holy.

Moses and Aaron were among His priests; Samuel also was among those who called on His name; they cried to the Lord, and He answered them.

He spoke to them in the pillar of cloud; they kept His testimonies and the statutes that He gave them.

O Lord our God, You heard them; You were
a forgiving God to them but an avenger of
their wrongdoings.

Extol the Lord our God and worship at His
holy mountain; for the Lord our God
is holy!

PSALM 100 (99)

Make a joyful noise to the Lord, all the
earth!

Serve the Lord with gladness! Come before
His Face with exultation.

Know that the Lord is God! It is He who
made us and not we ourselves; we are His
people and the sheep of His pasture.

Enter into His gates with thanksgiving and
His courts with praise; give thanks to
Him, praise His name!

For the Lord is good; His mercy endures
forever, and His truth from generation to
generation.

PSALM 101 (100)

I will sing of mercy and of justice; to You,
O Lord, I will sing a psalm.

I will have understanding of the perfect
way; when will You come to me?
I have walked with integrity of heart within
my house;
I have not set before my eyes anything that
is base; I hated the work of those who
fall away.
The perverse of heart did not cleave to
me; the evil man fled from me; I had no
dealings with him.
Him who slanders his neighbor secretly I
drove away;
I did not eat with the man of haughty looks
and greedy heart.
I looked with favor on the faithful in the
land, that they may dwell with me.
He who walks in the way that is blameless
ministered to me.
No man who acts pridefully dwelt in my
house;
no man who utters lies continued in my
presence.
Morning by morning I destroyed all the
wicked in the land, cutting off all the
evildoers from the city of the Lord.

KATHISMA 14—STASIS I

PSALM 102 (101)

Hear my prayer, O Lord; let my cry come
to You!

Do not turn Your Face from me in the day
of my distress!

Incline Your ear to me; hear me speedily in
the day when I call!

For my days have vanished like smoke, and
my bones have been parched like a stick.

I am blighted like grass, and my heart is
withered, for I have forgotten to eat my
bread.

Because of my loud groaning, my bones
cleave to my flesh.

I have become like a pelican of the
wilderness, like an owl in a ruined house.

I have watched and have become like a
lonely sparrow on the housetop.

All the day my enemies taunt me; those who
praised me have sworn against me.

For I have eaten ashes like bread and mingle
   tears with my drink because of Your
   indignation and anger; for You have taken
   me up and thrown me away.
My days have declined like a shadow; I
   wither away like grass.
But You, O Lord, endure forever; Your
   memory is from generation to generation.
You will arise and have mercy on Zion; it
   is time to have mercy on her; the time
   has come.
For Your servants hold her stones dear and
   have pity on her dust.
The nations will fear the name of the Lord,
   and all the kings of the earth Your glory.
For the Lord will build up Zion; He will
   appear in His glory; He has regarded the
   prayer of the humble and has not despised
   their supplication.
Let this be recorded for a generation to
   come, so that a people yet uncreated shall
   praise the Lord:
for He has looked down from His holy
   height; from heaven the Lord looked at
   the earth

to hear the groans of the prisoners, to set
    free the sons of those who were slain,

to declare the name of the Lord in Zion,
    and in Jerusalem His praise,

when peoples gather together, and kings, to
    serve the Lord.

Man asked the Lord in the course of his
    strength, "Make me to know the shortness
    of my days."

Take me not away in the midst of my
    days: Your years endure throughout all
    generations!

You, O Lord, in the beginning laid the
    foundation of the earth, and the heavens
    are the work of Your hands.

They will perish, but You remain; and they
    will all grow old like a garment; like a
    cloak You will fold them up, and they will
    be changed.

But You are the same, and Your years will
    not fail.

The children of Your servants shall dwell
    securely; their seed shall be led forever in
    the way of righteousness.

Bless the Lord, O my soul; and all that is
within me, bless His holy name!

Bless the Lord, O my soul, and forget not all
His benefits,

who forgives all your iniquity, who heals all
your diseases,

who redeems your life from the pit, who
crowns you with steadfast love and mercy,

who satisfies you with good as long as you
live, so that your youth is renewed like
the eagle's.

The Lord works vindication and justice for
all who are oppressed.

He made known His ways to Moses, His
acts to the people of Israel.

The Lord is compassionate and merciful,
long-suffering and of great goodness.

He will not always chide, nor will He keep
His anger forever.

He does not deal with us according to
our sins nor requite us according to our
iniquities.

For as the heavens are high above the earth,
so great is His steadfast love toward those
who fear Him;

as far as the east is from the west, so far
does He remove our transgressions
from us.

As a father pities his children, so the Lord
pities those who fear Him.

For He knows our frame; He remembers
that we are dust.

As for man, his days are like grass; he
flourishes like a flower of the field;

for the wind passes over it, and it is gone,
and its place knows it no more.

But the steadfast love of the Lord is from
everlasting to everlasting upon those
who fear Him, and His righteousness to
children's children,

to those who keep His covenant and
remember to do His commandments.

The Lord has established His throne in the
heavens, and His kingdom rules over all.

Bless the Lord, O you His angels,
you mighty ones who do His word,
hearkening to the voice of His word!

Bless the Lord, all His hosts, His ministers
that do His will!

Bless the Lord, all His works, in all places of
His dominion.

Bless the Lord, O my soul! In all places of
His dominion. Bless the Lord, O my soul!

✠ ✠ ✠

KATHISMA 14—STASIS II

PSALM 104 (103)

Bless the Lord, O my soul. O Lord, my
God, You are very great.

You are clothed with honor and majesty,
who cover Yourself with light as with a
garment;

who have stretched out the heavens like
a tent.

Who have laid the beams of Your chambers
on the waters,

who make the clouds Your chariot, who ride
on the wings of the wind.

Who make Your angels spirits and Your
ministers a fiery flame.

You set the earth on its foundations so that
it should never be shaken.

You covered it with the deep as with a
garment;

the waters stood above the mountains.

At Your rebuke they fled; at the sound of
Your thunder they took to flight.

The mountains rose; the valleys sank
down to the place which You appointed
for them.

You set a boundary which they should not
pass, so that they might not again cover
the earth.

You make springs gush forth in the valleys;
they flow between the hills.

They give drink to every beast of the field;
the wild asses quench their thirst.

By them the birds of the air have their
habitation; they sing among the branches.

From Your lofty abode You water the
mountains; the earth is satisfied with the
fruit of Your work.

You caused the grass to grow for the cattle, fodder for the animals that serve man.

That He may bring forth food from the earth, and wine to gladden the heart of man,

oil to make his face shine, and bread to strengthen man's heart.

The trees of the Lord are watered abundantly, the cedars of Lebanon which He planted.

In them the birds build their nests; the stork has her home in the fir trees.

The high mountains are for the wild goats; the rocks are a refuge for the badgers.

You have made the moon to mark the seasons. The sun knows its time for setting.

You make darkness, and it is night, when all the beasts of the forest creep forth.

The young lions roar for their prey, seeking their food from God.

When the sun rises, they get them away and lie down in their dens.

Man goes forth to his work and to his labor until the evening.

O Lord, how manifold are Your works. In wisdom have You made them all. The earth is full of Your creatures.

Yonder is the sea, great and wide, which teems with things innumerable, living things both small and great.

There go the ships, and Leviathan which You formed to sport in it.

These all look to You, to give them their food in due season.

When You give to them, they gather it up;

when You open Your hand, they are filled with good things.

When You hide Your Face, they are dismayed; when You take away their spirit, they die and return to their dust.

When You send forth Your Spirit, they are created, and You renew the face of the earth.

May the glory of the Lord endure forever. May the Lord rejoice in His works.

Who looks on the earth and it trembles; who touches the mountains and they smoke.

I will sing to the Lord as long as I live; I will
    sing praises to my God while I have being.
May my meditation be pleasing to Him, for
    I rejoice in the Lord.
Let sinners be consumed from the earth,
    and let the wicked be no more.
Bless the Lord, O my soul. Praise the Lord!

✠ ✠ ✠

KATHISMA 14—STASIS III

PSALM 105 (104)

O give thanks to the Lord, call on His
    name; make known His deeds among the
    peoples!
Sing to Him, sing praises to Him; tell of all
    His wonderful works!
Glory in His holy name; let the hearts of
    those who seek the Lord rejoice!
Seek the Lord and He will give You
    strength; seek His Face continually.

Remember the wonderful works that He
   has done, His miracles, and the judgments
   He uttered,
O offspring of Abraham His servant, sons of
   Jacob, His chosen ones!
He is the Lord our God; His judgments are
   in all the earth.
He is mindful of His covenant forever,
   of the word that He commanded, for a
   thousand generations,
the covenant which He made with
   Abraham,
His sworn promise to Isaac, which He
   confirmed to Jacob as a statute, to Israel as
   an everlasting covenant, saying,
"To you I will give the land of Canaan as
   your portion for an inheritance."
When they were few in number, of little
   account and foreigners in the land,
wandering from nation to nation, from one
   kingdom to another people,
He allowed no one to oppress them; He
   rebuked kings on their account, saying,
"Touch not those whom I have anointed; do
   my prophets no harm!"

He summoned a famine on the land and
   broke every staff of bread.
He sent a man ahead of them; Joseph was
   sold as a slave.
His feet were hurt with fetters; his neck was
   put in a collar of iron
until His word came to pass; the word of the
   Lord tested him like fire.
The king sent and released him; the ruler of
   the peoples set him free;
he made him lord of his house and ruler of
   all his possessions,
to instruct his princes at his pleasure and to
   teach his elders wisdom.
Then Israel came to Egypt; Jacob sojourned
   in the land of Ham.
And the Lord made His people very fruitful
   and made them stronger than their foes.
He turned their hearts to hate His people, to
   deal craftily with His servants.
He sent Moses His servant and Aaron whom
   He had chosen.
They wrought His signs among them and
   miracles in the land of Ham.

He sent darkness and made the land dark;
  yet they rebelled against His words.
He turned their waters into blood and
  caused their fish to die.
Their land swarmed with frogs, even in the
  chambers of the kings;
He spoke, and there came swarms of flies
  and gnats throughout their country.
He gave them hail for rain and lightning
  that flashed through their land.
He smote their vines and fig trees and
  shattered the trees of their country.
He spoke and the locusts came, and young
  locusts without number,
which devoured all the vegetation in their
  land and ate up the fruit of their ground.
He smote all the firstborn in their land, the
  first fruits of all their labor.
Then He led them forth with silver and
  gold, and there was not a feeble one
  among their tribes.
Egypt was glad when they departed, for
  dread of them had fallen upon it.
He spread a cloud as a covering for them
  and fire to give light by night.

They asked, and the quail came, and He
satisfied them with the bread of heaven.

He opened the rock, and water gushed
forth; it flowed through the desert like
a river.

For He remembered His holy word to
Abraham His servant.

So He led forth His people with joy, His
chosen ones with exultation.

And He gave them the lands of the nations;
and they took possession of the fruit of
the people's toil,

to the end that they should keep His
statutes, and diligently seek His laws.

✠ ✠ ✠

PSALM 106 (105)

O give thanks to the Lord, for He is good;
for His mercy endures forever.

Who shall utter the mighty doings of the
Lord or make all His praises to be heard?

Blessed are those who keep judgment and
do righteousness at all times!

Remember us, O Lord, with the favor you
show to Your people; visit us with Your
salvation,

that we may see the prosperity of Your
chosen ones; that we may rejoice in the
gladness of Your nation; that we may
glory with Your heritage.

We have sinned with our fathers; we have
transgressed; we have done unrighteously.

Our fathers, when they were in Egypt, did
not understand Your wonders;

they did not remember the abundance of
Your mercy but provoked You as they
went up by the Red Sea.

Yet He saved them for His name's sake, that
    He might make known His mighty power.

He rebuked the Red Sea, and it became
    dry; so He led them through the deep as
    through a desert.

He saved them from the hand of those who
    hated them and redeemed them from the
    hand of the enemy.

The waters covered their oppressors; not
    one of them was left.

Then they believed His words and
    celebrated His praise.

But they made haste to forget His works;
    they did not wait to know His counsel.

They had a wanton craving in the
    wilderness and tempted God in the
    waterless land;

He gave them what they asked and sent
    fullness into their souls.

They provoked Moses in the camp, and
    Aaron, the holy one of the Lord;

the earth opened and swallowed up Dathan
    and covered the company of Abiram.

A fire was kindled in their midst; a flame
    burned up the sinners.

They made a calf in Horeb and worshiped
  the graven image;
they exchanged their Glory for the likeness
  of a calf that eats grass.
They forgot God, who saved them, who had
  done great deeds in Egypt,
wondrous works in the land of Ham and
  terrible things by the Red Sea.
Therefore, He said, He would have
  destroyed them, had not Moses,
  His chosen one, stood in the breach
  before Him,
to turn away the fierceness of His wrath so
  that He should not destroy them.
But they despised the pleasant land and did
  not believe His word.
They murmured in their tents and did not
  listen to the voice of the Lord.
Therefore He raised His hand against them
  to cast them down in the wilderness,
and to cast down their seed among the
  nations, and to scatter them in the lands.
They were attached also to the Baal of Peor
  and ate the sacrifices of the dead;

and they provoked the Lord with their
doings, and destruction was multiplied
among them.

Then Phineas stood up and obtained
forgiveness, and the plague was stayed.

And that was reckoned to him as
righteousness from generation to
generation forever.

They provoked Him also at the waters
of Strife, and Moses was hurt on their
account;

for they provoked his spirit, and he spoke
words that were rash.

They did not destroy the peoples, as the
Lord commanded them, but they mingled
with the nations and learned to do as
they did.

They served their graven images, which
became a snare to them.

They sacrificed their sons and their
daughters to the demons;

they poured out innocent blood, the blood
of their sons and daughters, whom they
sacrificed to the idols of Canaan;

the land was polluted with blood and
became unclean by their acts; they played
the harlot in their doings.

Therefore the anger of the Lord was
kindled against His people, and He
abhorred His heritage;

He gave them into the hands of the
nations, and those who hated them ruled
over them.

Their enemies oppressed them, and they
were brought into subjection under their
hands.

Many times He delivered them, but they
provoked Him by their counsel and were
brought low through their iniquities.

Nevertheless, the Lord regarded their
distress when He heard their petition.

He remembered His covenant and relented
according to the abundance of His mercy.

He caused them to be pitied in the sight of
all those who carried them away captive.

Save us, O Lord our God, and gather us
from among the nations,

that we may confess Your holy name and
glory in praising You.

Blessed be the Lord, the God of Israel, from
everlasting to everlasting!
And all the people shall say, "Amen! Amen!"

✠ ✠ ✠

KATHISMA 15—STASIS II

PSALM 107 (106)

O give thanks to the Lord, for He is good;
for His mercy endures forever!
Let the redeemed of the Lord say so, whom
He has redeemed from the hand of the
enemy
and gathered in from the lands, from the
east and from the west, from the north
and from the south.
They wandered in the desert, in a waterless
land, without finding the city they were
to dwell in;
hungry and thirsty, their soul fainted
within them.

Then they cried to the Lord in their
trouble, and He delivered them from their
distresses;

He led them to a straight way, that they
might reach the city they were to dwell in.

Let them confess the Lord for His mercies
and His wonderful works to the sons
of men;

for He satisfies the thirsty, and the hungry
He fills with good things.

They were sitting in darkness and the
shadow of death, chained in poverty and
in irons,

because they had rebelled against the words
of God and had despised the counsel of
the Most High.

So their hearts were bowed down with
labors; they were weak, and there was no
helper.

Then they cried to the Lord in their
trouble, and He delivered them from their
distresses;

He brought them out of darkness and the
shadow of death and broke their bonds
asunder.

Let them confess the Lord for His mercies
and His wonderful works to the sons
of men!

For He shattered the doors of bronze and
crushed the bars of iron.

He helped them out of their sinful way, for
they were brought low because of their
iniquities;

their soul loathed all food, and they drew
near to the gates of death.

Then they cried to the Lord in their
trouble, and He delivered them from their
distresses;

He sent forth His Word and healed them,
and delivered them from their corruption.

Let them confess the Lord for His mercies
and His wonderful works to the sons
of men!

And let them offer to Him the sacrifice
of praise and tell of His deeds with
exultation!

Those who go down to the sea in ships,
doing business on many waters,

have seen the deeds of the Lord and His
wondrous works in the deep.

He spoke, and the stormy wind arose, and
its waves were lifted up.

They mounted up to the heavens, they went
down to the depths; their souls melted
away because of their troubles;

they reeled and staggered like drunken
men, and all their wisdom was
swallowed up.

Then they cried to the Lord in their
trouble, and He delivered them from their
distress;

and He commanded the storm, and it was
calmed to a gentle breeze, and its waves
were stilled.

Then they were glad because they had quiet,
and He guided them to their desired
haven.

Let them confess the Lord for His mercies
and His wonderful works to the sons
of men!

Let them extol Him in the congregation of
the people and praise Him in the council
of the elders.

For He turned rivers into a desert, springs
of water into thirsty ground, and a

fruitful land into a salty waste because of the wickedness of its inhabitants.

He turned the desert into pools of water, parched land into springs of water.

And there He settled the hungry, and they established the city they were to dwell in.

They sowed fields, and planted vineyards, and gathered fruits of all sorts.

He blessed them, and they multiplied greatly; and He did not let their flocks decrease.

But afterward they were diminished and brought low through the afflictions of tribulation and suffering.

Contempt was poured upon their princes, and He made them wander in a desert and trackless waste;

but He helped the poor out of poverty and made their families like a flock.

The upright shall see and be glad, and all wickedness shall stop its mouth.

Who is wise to give heed to these things and understand the mercy of the Lord?

✠ ✠ ✠

PSALM 108 (107)

My heart, O God, is ready, my heart is
  ready. I will sing, yes, I will sing psalms!

Awake, O my soul! Awake, O harp and lyre!
  I will awake the dawn!

I will confess You, O Lord, among the
  peoples; I will sing praises to You among
  the nations.

For Your mercy is higher than the heavens,
  and Your truth reaches to the clouds.

Be exalted, O God, above the heavens, and
  Your glory over all the earth!

That Your beloved may be delivered, save
  by Your right hand and hear me!

God has spoken in His sanctuary: "I will be
  exalted and will divide up Shechem and
  portion out the valley of Succoth.

Gilead is Mine and Manasseh is Mine;
  Ephraim is the protection of My head;
  Judah is My king.

Moab is My washbasin; upon Edom I will
  cast My shoe; the Philistines are subjected
  to Me."

Who will bring me to the fortified city?
Who will lead me to Edom?

Will not You, O God, although You have
rejected us? Will not You, O God, go
forth with our armies?

Oh, grant us help in times of tribulation, for
vain is the help of man!

With God we shall do valiantly; it is He
who will bring our foes down to nothing.

PSALM 109 (108)

O God, do not pass over my praise in
silence!

For the mouth of the wicked and the mouth
of the deceitful are opened against me,
speaking against me with lying tongues.

They beset me with words of hate and
attack me without cause.

In return for my love, they falsely accused
me, but I continued to pray for them.

They rewarded me evil for good and hatred
for my love.

And they say, "Appoint a sinner against him;
let the Accuser stand at his right hand.

When he is tried, let him come forth condemned; let his prayer be counted as sin.

May his days be few; may another seize his high office.

May his children be fatherless and his wife a widow.

May his sons wander without a dwelling and beg; may they be driven out of the ruins they inhabit.

May the creditor seize all that he has; may strangers plunder the fruit of his toil.

Let him have no helper, nor anyone to pity his fatherless children.

May his children be utterly destroyed; may his name be blotted out in one generation.

May the iniquity of his fathers be remembered before the Lord, and let not the sin of his mother be blotted out; let them be before the Lord continually.

And may their memory be cut off from the earth.

For he did not remember to show mercy but persecuted the poor and needy and the brokenhearted to their death.

He loved to curse; let curses come on him!

He did not like blessing; may it be far
from him!

He clothed himself with cursing as his coat;
may it soak into his body like water, like
oil into his bones.

May it be like a garment which he wraps
round him, like a belt with which he
continually girds himself."

This is the work of those who falsely accuse
me before the Lord, of those who speak
evil against my soul.

But You, O Lord, deal mercifully with me
for Your name's sake, for Your mercy
is good.

Deliver me, for I am poor and needy, and
my heart is stricken within me.

I am gone, like a shadow at evening; I am
shaken off like a locust.

My knees are weak through fasting; my
body has become gaunt for lack of oil.

I am a reproach to them; when they see me,
they wag their heads.

Help me, O Lord my God! Save me
according to Your mercy,

that they may know that this is Your hand;
that You, O Lord, have done it!

Let them curse, but You shall bless.

Let my assailants be put to shame; let Your
servant be glad!

Let those who falsely accuse me be clothed
with dishonor; may they be wrapped in
their own shame as in a mantle!

With a loud voice, I will confess the Lord;
I will praise Him in the midst of the
throng.

For He stands at the right hand of the poor
man to save my soul from those who
persecute me.

✠ ✠ ✠

PSALM 135 (134)

Praise the name of the Lord; give praise,
O servants of the Lord,

You that stand in the house of the Lord, in
the courts of the house of our God.

Praise the Lord, for the Lord is good; sing
to His name, for He is gracious,

For the Lord has chosen Jacob for Himself,
Israel as His own possession.

For I know that the Lord is great and that
our Lord is above all gods.

Whatever the Lord pleases, He does, in
heaven and on earth, in the seas and
all deeps.

He it is who makes the clouds rise at the end
of the earth,

who makes lightning for the rain and brings
forth the wind from His storehouses.

He it was who smote the firstborn of Egypt,
both of man and of beast;

Who in your midst, O Egypt, sent signs
and wonders against Pharaoh and all his
servants.

Who smote many nations and slew mighty
kings—

Sihon, King of the Amorites, and Og, King
of Bashan,

and all the kingdoms of Canaan, and gave
their land as a heritage, a heritage to His
people Israel.

Your name, O Lord, endures forever, Your
renown, O Lord, throughout all ages.

For the Lord will vindicate His people and
have compassion on His servants.

The idols of the nations are silver and gold,
the work of men's hands.

They have mouths, but they speak not; they
have eyes, but they see not.

They have ears, but they hear not, nor is
there any breath in their mouths.

Let those who make them be like them—
yea, everyone who trusts in them.

O house of Israel, bless the Lord. O house
of Aaron, bless the Lord.

O house of Levi, bless the Lord; you that
fear the Lord, bless the Lord.

Blessed be the Lord from Zion, He who
dwells in Jerusalem. Alleluia.

PSALM 136 (135)

O give thanks to the Lord, for He is good;
O give thanks to the God of gods;

O give thanks to the Lord of lords, for His
steadfast love endures forever.

To Him who alone does great wonders, to
Him who by understanding made the
heavens, for His steadfast love endures
forever.

To Him who spread out the earth upon the
waters, to Him who made the great lights,
for His steadfast love endures forever.

The sun to rule over the day, the moon
and stars to rule over the night, for His
steadfast love endures forever.

To Him who smote the firstborn of Egypt
and brought Israel out from among them,

with a strong hand and an outstretched arm,
for His steadfast love endures forever.

To Him who divided the Red Sea asunder
and made Israel pass through the midst
of it,

But overthrew Pharaoh and his host in the
Red Sea, for His steadfast love endures
forever.

To Him who led His people through the
wilderness, to Him who smote great kings

And slew famous kings, for His steadfast
love endures forever.

Sihon, King of the Amorites, and Og, King
of Bashan, for His steadfast love endures
forever.

And gave their land as a heritage, a heritage
to Israel His servant, for His steadfast love
endures forever.

It is He who remembered us in our low
estate and rescued us from our foes,

He who gives food to all flesh, for His
steadfast love endures forever.

O give thanks to the God of heaven, for His
steadfast love endures forever. Alleluia.

By the waters of Babylon, there we sat
down and wept when we remembered
Zion.

On the willows there we hung up our lyres.

For there our captors required of us sacred
songs, and those who led us away, hymns,
saying, "Sing us one of the songs of Zion."

How shall we sing the Lord's song in a
foreign land?

If I forget you, O Jerusalem, let my right
hand be forgotten!

Let my tongue cleave to my throat if I
do not remember you, if I do not set
Jerusalem above my highest joy!

Remember, O Lord, the sons of Edom in
the day of Jerusalem, who said, "Raze it,
raze it, down to its foundations!"

O wretched daughter of Babylon, blessed
shall he be who repays you with what you
have done to us!

Blessed shall he be who takes your little
ones and dashes them against the rock!

✠ ✠ ✠

PSALM 138 (137)

I will give You thanks, O Lord, with my
whole heart; before the angels I will sing
psalms to You,

for You have heard all the words of my
mouth;

I will worship toward Your holy temple and
confess Your name for Your mercy and
Your truth;

for You have exalted above everything Your
holy name.

On the day I call upon You, hear me; in
Your strength, You will multiply Your
care for my soul.

Let all the kings of the earth confess You,
O Lord, for they have heard all the words
of Your mouth;

and let them sing of the ways of the Lord,
for great is the glory of the Lord.

For though the Lord is high, He regards
the lowly; but the haughty He knows
from afar.

If I walk in the midst of trouble, You will
give me life;
You have stretched out Your hand against
the wrath of my enemies, and Your right
hand delivered me.
O Lord, you will fulfill Your purpose
for me;
Your mercy, O Lord, endures forever. Do
not despise the works of Your hands.

PSALM 139 (138)

O Lord, You have tested me and
known me!
You know when I lie down and when
I awake; You discern my thoughts
from afar.
You have known my path and the extent of
my life, and have foreseen all my ways,
that there is no unrighteous word on my
tongue.
Lo, O Lord, You know all things: the last
and the first.
You have fashioned me and laid Your hand
upon me.

Your knowledge is too wonderful for me; it
is high, I cannot attain it.

Where shall I go from Your Spirit? And
where shall I flee from Your Face?

If I ascend to heaven, You are there! If I go
down to Sheol, You are there!

If I take my wings toward the morning and
dwell in the uttermost parts of the sea,

even there Your hand shall lead me, and
Your right hand shall hold me.

And I said, "Surely the darkness will cover
me," but even the night itself became light
in my joy.

For darkness will not be dark to You,
but the night will be bright as the day;
darkness will be as light.

For You, O Lord, formed my inward parts;
You knitted me together in my mother's
womb.

I will give thanks to You, for I am fearfully
and wondrously made.

Marvelous are Your works, and my
soul knows it in a manner beyond
understanding!

My bones which You made in secret were
not hidden from You, nor my substance
in the depths of the earth.

Your eyes beheld my unformed substance,

and in Your book they all were written, the
days that You were yet to make, and none
of them were missing.

Your friends are greatly honored in my eyes,
O God; their rule is very great!

I will count them, and they will be
multiplied more than the sand.

When I awake, I am still with You.

O that You would slay the wicked, O God!

Depart from me, O men of blood, for you
are quarrelsome in your thoughts.

It is in vain that they will take Your cities,
O Lord.

Have I not hated those who hate You? And
have I not wasted away from zeal because
of Your enemies?

I hated them with perfect hatred; they
became my enemies.

Test me, O God, and know my heart! Try
me and know my paths!

And see if there be any wicked way in me,
and lead me in the way everlasting!

PSALM 140 (139)

Deliver me, O Lord, from evil men; rescue
me from violent men

who plot iniquity in their heart and stir up
wars all the day.

They have made their tongue sharp as
a serpent's, and under their lips is the
poison of vipers.

Guard me, O Lord, from the hand of the
sinner; deliver me from violent men who
have planned to overthrow my steps.

Arrogant men have hidden a trap for me,
and with cords they have spread a net;
by the wayside they have set a stumbling
block for me.

I say to the Lord, "You are my God; give ear
to the voice of my supplications, O Lord!"

Lord, O Lord, the strength of my salvation,
You will cover my head in the day of
battle.

According to my desires, O Lord, do not
hand me over to the wicked.

They have taken counsel against me; do not
forsake me, lest they be exalted.

On the heads of those who surround me
will fall the mischief of their lips!

Burning coals will fall upon them; You
will cast them down into the fire, into
unbearable afflictions.

A gossip will not prosper in the land; evils
will hunt down the unrighteous man to
destruction.

I know that the Lord will maintain the
cause of the poor and the right of the
needy.

Surely the righteous will give thanks to
Your name; the upright will dwell before
Your Face.

✠ ✠ ✠

KATHISMA 19—STASIS III

PSALM 141 (140)

Lord, I call upon You; hear me. Hear me,
O Lord.

Lord, I call upon You; hear me. Receive the
voice of my prayer when I call upon You.

Let my prayer arise in Your sight as incense,
and let the lifting up of my hands be an
evening sacrifice. Hear me, O Lord.

Set a guard over my mouth, O Lord; keep
watch over the door of my lips!

Incline not my heart to any evil, to busy
myself with wicked deeds in company
with men who work iniquity; and let me
not partake of their delights!

Let a good man strike or rebuke me in
kindness, but let the oil of the wicked
never anoint my head, for my prayer is
continually against their wicked deeds.

When they are given over to those who
shall condemn them, then they shall learn
that the word of the Lord is true.

As a rock which one cleaves and shatters on
the land, so shall their bones be strewn at
the mouth of Sheol.

But my eyes are toward You, O Lord
God; in You I seek refuge; leave me not
defenseless!

Keep me from the trap which they have laid
for me and from the snares of evildoers!

Let the wicked together fall into their own
nets, while I escape.

PSALM 142 (141)

I cry with my voice to the Lord; with my
voice I make supplication to the Lord.

I pour out my complaint before Him; I tell
my trouble before Him.

When my spirit is faint, You know my way.

In the path where I walk they have hidden a
trap for me.

I look to the right and watch, but there is
none who takes notice of me;

no refuge remains to me, no man cares
for me.

I cry to You, O Lord; I say, "You are my
refuge, my portion in the land of the
living."

Give heed to my cry, for I am brought
very low!

Deliver me from my persecutors, for they
are too strong for me.

Bring my soul out of prison, that I may give
thanks to Your name!

The righteous will surround me, for You
will deal bountifully with me.

PSALM 143 (142)

Hear my prayer, O Lord; give ear to my
supplications! In Your faithfulness answer
me, in Your righteousness!

Enter not into judgment with Your servant;
for no man living is righteous before You.

For the enemy has pursued me; he has
crushed my life to the ground; he has
made me sit in darkness like those
long dead.

Therefore my spirit faints within me; my
heart within me is appalled.

I remember the days of old; I meditate on
all that You have done; I muse on what
Your hands have wrought.

I stretch out my hands to You; my soul
thirsts for You like a parched land.

Make haste to answer me, O Lord! My
spirit fails!

Hide not Your Face from me, lest I be like
those who go down to the Pit.
Let me hear in the morning of Your
steadfast love, for in You I put my trust.
Teach me the way I should go, for to You I
lift up my soul.
Deliver me, O Lord, from my enemies! I
have fled to You for refuge!
Teach me to do Your will, for You are
my God.
Let Your good Spirit lead me on a
level path.
For Your name's sake, O Lord, preserve my
life. In Your righteousness bring me out
of trouble.
And in Your steadfast love cut off my
enemies and destroy all my adversaries,
for I am Your servant.

✠ ✠ ✠

PSALM 144 (143)

Blessed be the Lord my God, who trains
my hands for war and my fingers for
battle;

my mercy and my refuge, my helper and my
deliverer,

my protector in whom I have trusted, who
subdues the peoples under me.

O Lord, what is man that You make
Yourself known to him, or the son of man
that You take him into account?

Man is like vanity; his days are like a
passing shadow.

Bow Your heavens, O Lord, and come
down! Touch the mountains, and they
shall smoke!

Flash forth the lightning and scatter them;
send out Your arrows and rout them!

Stretch forth Your hand from on high;
rescue me and deliver me from the many
waters,

from the hands of the sons of strangers,
whose mouths speak vanity and
whose right hand is a right hand of
unrighteousness.

I will sing a new song to You, O God; upon
a ten-stringed harp I will play to You,

to You who give victory to kings, who
rescued David Your servant from the
cruel sword.

Deliver me and rescue me from the hands
of the sons of strangers, whose mouths
speak vanity and whose right hand is a
right hand of unrighteousness.

Their sons are strengthened in their
youth like plants; their daughters are
made beautiful, richly adorned like the
structure of a palace.

Their garners are full, overflowing with all
manner of store;

their sheep are prolific, multiplying in their
folds; their oxen are fat.

There is no breach or fissure in their walls,
nor any outcry in their squares.

They have called people who are like this
blessed, but blessed are the people whose
God is the Lord!

PSALM 145 (144)

I will extol You, my God and King, and
bless Your name forever and ever.
Every day I will bless You and praise Your
name forever and ever.
Great is the Lord, and greatly to be praised,
and His greatness is unsearchable.
One generation shall laud Your works
to another and shall declare Your
mighty acts.
They shall speak of the glorious splendor of
Your holiness and recount Your wondrous
works.
Men shall proclaim the might of Your
terrible acts and declare Your greatness.
They shall pour forth the fame of Your
abundant goodness and shall sing aloud of
Your righteousness.
The Lord is compassionate and merciful,
long-suffering and abounding in mercy.

The Lord is good to all, and His
compassions are over all that He has made.

Let all Your works give thanks to You,
O Lord, and let Your saints bless You!

They shall speak of the glory of Your
kingdom and tell of Your power,

to make known to the sons of men Your
power and the glorious splendor of Your
kingdom.

Your kingdom is an everlasting kingdom,
and Your dominion endures throughout
all generations.

The Lord is true in all His words and holy
in all His works.

The Lord upholds all who are falling and
raises up all who are bowed down.

The eyes of all look to You, and You give
them their food in due season.

You open Your hand; You fill every living
thing with blessing.

The Lord is righteous in all His ways and
holy in all His works.

The Lord is near to all who call upon Him,
to all who call upon Him in truth.

He will fulfill the desire of those who fear
Him, and He will hear their cry and
save them.

The Lord preserves all who love Him, but
all the wicked He will destroy.

My mouth will speak the praise of the
Lord, and let all flesh bless His holy name
forever and ever.

✠ ✠ ✠

KATHISMA 20—STASIS II

PSALM 146 (145)

Praise the Lord! Praise the Lord,
O my soul!

I will praise the Lord as long as I live; I will
sing praises to my God while I have being.

Put not your trust in princes, in sons of
men, in whom there is no salvation.

When his breath departs, he returns to his
earth; on that very day his plans perish.

Blessed is he whose help is the God of Jacob,
whose hope is in the Lord his God,

who made heaven and earth, the sea, and all
that is in them;

who keeps faith forever; who executes
justice for the oppressed; who gives food
to the hungry.

The Lord sets the prisoners free; the Lord
opens the eyes of the blind.

The Lord lifts up those who are bowed
down; the Lord loves the righteous.

The Lord watches over the sojourners; He
upholds the widow and the fatherless; but
the way of the wicked He brings to ruin.

The Lord will reign forever, Your God, O
Zion, to all generations. Praise the Lord!

PSALM 147 (146 & 147)

Praise the Lord, for it is good to sing
praises to our God. Let our praises be
pleasing to Him!

The Lord builds up Jerusalem; He gathers
the outcasts of Israel.

He heals the brokenhearted and binds up
their wounds.

He determines the number of the stars; He
calls them all by name.

Great is our God and abundant in power.
His understanding is beyond measure!

The Lord lifts up the meek but casts the
sinners to the ground.

Intone a song of thanksgiving to the Lord;
sing praises upon the harp to our God!

Who covers the heavens with clouds, who
prepares rain for the earth,

Who makes grass grow upon the hills and
herbs for the use of men,

and gives to the beasts their food, and to the
young ravens which cry to Him.

His delight will not be in the strength of
the horse nor His pleasure in the legs of
a man;

but the Lord takes pleasure in those who
fear Him, in those who hope in His
mercy.

Praise the Lord, O Jerusalem! Praise your
God, O Zion!

For He strengthens the bars of your gates;
He blesses your sons within you.

He makes peace in your borders; He fills
you with the finest of the wheat.

He sends forth His word to the earth; His proclamation runs swiftly.

He gives snow like wool; He scatters the mist like ashes.

He casts forth His ice like crumbs; who shall stand before His cold?

He will send forth His word and melt them; He will blow with His Spirit and the waters will flow.

He declares His word to Jacob, His statutes and judgments to Israel.

He has not dealt thus with any other nation and has not shown His judgments to them.

☩ ☩ ☩

KATHISMA 20—STASIS III

PSALM 148

Praise the Lord! Praise the Lord from heaven, praise Him in the highest!

Praise Him, all you angels of His! Praise Him, all His hosts!

Praise Him, sun and moon; praise Him, all
you stars and light.
Praise Him, you highest heavens and you
waters above the heavens.
Let them praise the name of the Lord,
for He spoke and they came to be; He
commanded, and they were created.
He established them forever and ever; He
set a law which cannot pass away.
Praise the Lord from the earth, you sea
monsters and all deeps,
fire and hail, snow and frost, stormy winds
fulfilling His word.
Mountains and all hills, fruit trees and all
cedars,
beasts and all cattle, creeping things and
flying birds,
kings of the earth and all peoples, princes
and rulers of the earth,
young men and maidens together, old men
and children:
Let them praise the name of the Lord,
for His name alone is exalted; He is
acknowledged in heaven and on earth;

and He will raise up a horn for His people—
a song for all His saints, the sons of Israel
who are near to Him. Praise the Lord!

PSALM 149

Praise the Lord! Sing to the Lord a new
song, His praise in the church of the
faithful.

Let Israel be glad in his Maker; let the sons
of Zion rejoice in their King.

Let them praise His name with dancing,
making melody to Him with timbrel and
psalms.

For the Lord takes pleasure in His people
and exalts the humble in salvation.

Let the faithful exult in glory; let them sing
for joy on their beds.

Let the high praises of God be in their
throats and two-edged swords in their
hands,

to wreak vengeance on the nations and
chastisement on the peoples;

to bind their kings with chains and their
nobles with iron fetters,

to execute on them the judgment written;
  this is glory for all His saints.
Praise the Lord!

PSALM 150

Praise the Lord! Praise God in His
  sanctuary; praise Him in His mighty
  firmament.
Praise Him for His powers; praise Him
  according to His exceeding greatness.
Praise Him with trumpet sound; praise Him
  in psalms and harp.
Praise Him with timbrel and dance; praise
  Him with strings and pipe.
Praise Him with sounding cymbals; praise
  Him with loud clashing cymbals!
Let every breath praise the Lord! Praise
  the Lord!

✠ ✠ ✠

PSALM 120 (119)

In my distress I cried to the Lord, and He
   answered me:

"Deliver me, O Lord, from unjust lips and
   from a deceitful tongue."

What shall be given to you? And what
   more shall be done to you, you deceitful
   tongue?

Sharpened weapons of the Almighty;
   devastating glowing coals!

Woe is me, that my sojourning is prolonged,
   that I dwell among the tents of Kedar; my
   soul has long been in exile.

I was peaceful among those who hated
   peace; when I spoke to them, they fought
   against me without a cause.

PSALM 121 (120)

I lift up my eyes to the hills, from where
   my help will come.

My help comes from the Lord, who made
heaven and earth.
He will not let your foot be moved; He who
keeps you will not slumber.
Behold, He who keeps Israel will neither
slumber nor sleep.
The Lord will keep you; the Lord will be
your protection at your right hand.
The sun shall not smite you by day, nor the
moon by night.
May the Lord keep you from all evil; the
Lord will keep your soul.
The Lord will keep your going out and
your coming in from this time forth and
forevermore.

PSALM 122 (121)

I rejoiced when they said to me, "Let us go
to the house of the Lord!"
Our feet were standing within your gates,
O Jerusalem!
Jerusalem is built as a city whose features
are harmoniously composed.

For there the tribes went up, the tribes of
the Lord, as a decree for Israel, to give
thanks to the name of the Lord.
There thrones for judgment are set, the
thrones of the house of David.
Pray now for the peace of Jerusalem and for
prosperity for those who love you!
Let peace be in your strongholds and
prosperity within your palaces!
For my brethren and neighbors' sake, I have
spoken peace concerning you.
For the sake of the house of the Lord our
God, I have diligently sought your good.

PSALM 123 (122)

To You I lift up my eyes, who are
enthroned in the heavens!
Behold, as the eyes of servants look to the
hand of their master,
as the eyes of a maid to the hand of her
mistress,
so our eyes look to the Lord our God, till
He have mercy on us.

Have mercy on us, O Lord, have mercy on
us, for we have had more than enough of
contempt.

Too long our soul has been sated with
the scorn of those who are at ease, the
contempt of the proud.

PSALM 124 (123)

If it had not been that the Lord was among
us, let Israel now say,

if it had not been that the Lord was among
us, when men rose up against us,

they would indeed have swallowed us
up alive when their anger was kindled
against us;

indeed, the flood would have swept us
away; our soul would have gone under the
torrent;

indeed our soul would have gone under the
raging waters.

Blessed be the Lord, who has not given us as
prey to their teeth!

Our soul has been delivered like a bird
from the snare of the fowler; the snare is
broken, and we are delivered!

Our help is in the name of the Lord, who made heaven and earth!

KATHISMA 18—STASIS II

PSALM 125 (124)

Those who trust in the Lord are like Mount Zion. He that dwells in Jerusalem will never be shaken.

As the mountains are round about Jerusalem, so the Lord is round about His people, from this time forth and forevermore.

For the Lord will not allow the scepter of sinners to rest upon the lot of the righteous, lest the righteous put forth their hands to do wrong.

Do good, O Lord, to those who are good and to those who are upright in heart!

But those who turn aside upon their crooked ways the Lord will lead away with evildoers.

Peace be in Israel!

PSALM 126 (125)

When the Lord brought back the captives of Zion, we became like those who are comforted.

Then our mouth was filled with joy and our tongue with exultation;

then they said among the nations, "The Lord has done great things for them."

The Lord had done great things for us; we were filled with joy.

O Lord, bring back our captives like the streams in the south; those who sow in tears will reap in joy!

They went forth weeping as they sowed their seeds; but they will surely come with exultation, bringing their sheaves with them.

PSALM 127 (126)

Unless the Lord builds the house, those who build it labor in vain.

Unless the Lord watches over the city, the watchman stays awake in vain.

It is in vain that you rise up early, rising up
from rest, eating the bread of anxious toil;
for He gives to His beloved sleep.

Lo, children are a heritage from the Lord,
the fruit of the womb a reward.

Like arrows in the hand of a mighty man
are the sons of one's youth.

Blessed is the man who has his quiver full
of them!

He will not be put to shame when he speaks
with his enemies in the gate.

PSALM 128 (127)

Blessed are all those who fear the Lord,
those who walk in His ways!

You shall eat of the fruit of your labor;
you shall be blessed and filled with good
things.

Your wife shall be like a fruitful vine
within your house;

your children will be like olive shoots
around your table.

Lo, thus shall the man be blessed who fears
the Lord.

May the Lord bless you from Zion, and may
you see the good things of Jerusalem all
the days of your life!
And may you see your children's children!
Peace be upon Israel!

PSALM 129 (128)

"Often have they fought me from my
youth," let Israel now say.
"Often have they fought me from my
youth," yet they have not prevailed
against me.
The sinners worked upon my back; they
lengthened their wickedness.
The Lord is righteous; He has broken the
necks of the wicked.
May all who hate Zion be put to shame and
turned backward!
Let them be like the grass on the housetops,
which withers before it grows up,
with which the reaper does not fill his hand
or the binder of sheaves his bosom.
And those who pass by do not say, "The
blessing of the Lord be upon you! We
bless you in the name of the Lord!"

✠ ✠ ✠

KATHISMA 18—STASIS III

PSALM 130 (129)

Out of the depths I cry to You, O Lord.
Lord, hear my voice.

Let Your ears be attentive to the voice of my
supplication.

If You, O Lord, should mark iniquities,
Lord, who could stand?

But there is forgiveness with You, that You
may be feared.

For Your name's sake I have waited for You,
O Lord; my soul has hoped on the Lord.

From the morning watch until night, from
the morning watch, let Israel hope on
the Lord.

For with the Lord there is steadfast love,
and with Him is plenteous redemption,

and He will deliver Israel from all his
iniquities.

PSALM 131 (130)

O Lord, my heart is not lifted up; my eyes
    are not raised too high;
I did not delve into things too great and too
    marvelous for me.
If I have not kept my heart humble, but
    have lifted up my soul;
if I have not remained like a weaned child
    by his mother's side, let my soul receive its
    recompense.
Let Israel hope in the Lord from this time
    forth and forevermore.

PSALM 132 (131)

O Lord, remember David and all his
    meekness; how he swore to the Lord and
    vowed to the God of Jacob:
"I will not enter the tent of my house; I will
    not go up to the couch of my bed;
I will not give sleep to my eyes or slumber
    to my eyelids or rest to my temples,
until I find a place for the Lord, a dwelling
    place for the God of Jacob."

Lo, we heard of it in Ephratha; we found it
in the fields of the wood.

"Let us enter His dwelling place; let us
worship at the place where His feet
stood!"

Arise, O Lord, into Your resting place, You
and the ark of Your holiness!

Your priests will be clothed in
righteousness, and Your saints shall
rejoice.

For Your servant David's sake, do not turn
away the face of Your Anointed.

The Lord swore in truth to David, from
which He will not turn back:

"Of the fruit of your body, I will set upon
your throne.

If your sons will keep My covenant and My
testimonies which I shall teach them,

their sons also forever shall sit upon your
throne."

For the Lord has chosen Zion; He has
desired it for His habitation:

"This is my resting place forever; here I will
dwell, for I have desired it.

I will abundantly bless her provisions; I will
satisfy her poor with bread.

Her priests I will clothe with salvation, and
her saints will shout for joy.

There I will make a horn to sprout for
David; I have prepared a lamp for my
Anointed.

His enemies I will clothe with shame, but
upon Him my sanctification will flourish."

PSALM 133 (132)

Behold, how good and pleasant it is when
brothers dwell in unity.

It is like myrrh upon the head that runs
down the beard, the beard of Aaron, that
runs down the collar of his robe.

It is like the dew of Hermon which falls on
the mountains of Zion.

For there the Lord commanded the blessing:
life forevermore.

PSALM 134 (133)

Behold, now bless the Lord, all you
servants of the Lord,

you that stand in the house of the Lord, in
the courts of the house of our God.

Lift up your hands by night to the Holy of
Holies and bless the Lord!

May the Lord bless you from Zion, He who
made heaven and earth!

✠ ✠ ✠

PSALM 110 (109)

The Lord said to my Lord, "Sit at My right hand till I make Your enemies Your footstool."

The Lord sends forth from Zion Your mighty scepter. Rule in the midst of Your foes!

With You is dominion on the day of Your birth, in the radiance of holiness; out of the womb before the morning star have I begotten You.

The Lord has sworn and will not change His mind: You are a priest forever after the order of Melchizedek!

The Lord at Your right hand has shattered kings in the day of His wrath.

He will judge the nations, filling them with corpses; He will crush the heads of many on the earth.

He will drink from the brook by the way; therefore He will lift up his head.

I will confess You, O Lord, with my whole
heart in the company of the upright, in
the congregation; great are the works of
the Lord.

They are studied by all who have pleasure
in them.

His work is glory and beauty, and His
righteousness endures forever.

He has caused His wonderful works to be
remembered; the Lord is compassionate
and merciful.

He has provided food for those who fear
Him; He will always remember His
covenant.

He has declared to His people the power of
His works, to give them the heritage of
the peoples.

The works of His hands are truth
and judgment; all His precepts are
trustworthy;

they are established forever and ever,
performed in truth and uprightness.

The Lord has sent redemption to His people; He has commanded His covenant forever. Holy and terrible is His name!

The fear of the Lord is the beginning of wisdom; a good understanding have all those who practice it.

His praise endures forever and ever!

PSALM 112 (111)

Blessed is the man who fears the Lord, who greatly delights in His commandments!

His descendants will be mighty on the earth; the generation of the upright shall be blessed!

Glory and wealth are in his house, and his righteousness endures forever.

Light rises in the darkness for the upright; the Lord is merciful, compassionate, and righteous.

It is well with the man who deals mercifully and lends, who conducts his affairs with justice; for he will never be moved.

The righteous will be remembered forever; he is not afraid of evil tidings.

His heart is firm, trusting in the Lord; his
heart is steady; he will not be afraid until
he sees his enemies routed.

He has scattered freely abroad; he has given
to the poor; his righteousness endures
forever; his horn will be exalted in glory.

The sinner will see it and be angry; he
will gnash his teeth and wither away; the
desire of the sinner will perish.

✠ ✠ ✠

KATHISMA 16—STASIS II

PSALM 113 (112)

Praise the Lord, O you servants of the
Lord; praise the name of the Lord!

Blessed be the name of the Lord, henceforth
and forevermore.

From the rising of the sun to its setting, let
the name of the Lord be praised!

The Lord is exalted above all nations and
His glory above the heavens!

Who is like the Lord our God, who dwells
on high, who looks down upon the
heavens and the earth?
He raises the poor from the dust and lifts
the needy from the dunghill,
to set him with princes, with the princes of
His people.
He gives the barren woman a home, making
her the joyous mother of children.

PSALM 114 (113A)

When Israel went forth from Egypt, the
house of Jacob from a people of strange
language,
Judah became his sanctuary, Israel his
dominion.
The sea looked and fled; Jordan was
driven back.
The mountains skipped like rams, the hills
like lambs.
What ails you, O sea, that you flee?
O Jordan, that you turn back?
How is it, O mountains, that you skipped
like rams and you hills, like lambs?

The earth trembled before the Face of the
Lord, before the Face of the God of Jacob,
Who turned the rock into pools of water,
the flint into springs of water.

PSALM 115 (113B)

Not to us, O Lord, not to us, but to Your
name give glory, for the sake of Your
mercy and Your truth,
lest the nations should say, "Where is
their God?"
Our God is in heaven and on earth; He does
whatever He pleases.
The idols of the nations are silver and gold,
the works of men's hands.
They have mouths, but do not speak; eyes,
but do not see.
They have ears, but do not hear; noses, but
do not smell.
They have hands, but do not feel; feet, but
do not walk; and they do not make a
sound in their throat.
Let those who make them be like them, and
all who trust in them.

The house of Israel trusts in the Lord; He is
their helper and defender.

The house of Aaron trusts in the Lord; He
is their helper and defender.

Those who fear the Lord trust in the Lord;
He is their helper and defender.

The Lord has been mindful of us; He has
blessed us;

He has blessed the house of Israel; He has
blessed the house of Aaron;

He has blessed those who fear the Lord,
both small and great.

May the Lord give you increase, you and
your children!

May you be blessed by the Lord, who made
heaven and earth!

The heavens are the Lord's heavens, but the
earth He has given to the sons of men.

The dead will not praise the Lord, nor any
that go down into Sheol.

But we who live will bless the Lord from
this time forth and forevermore.

I love the Lord because He has heard the
voice of my supplication.

Because He inclined His ear to me,
therefore I will call on Him as long as
I live.

The snares of death encompassed me; the
pangs of Sheol laid hold on me;

I suffered distress and anguish; then I called
upon the name of the Lord: "O Lord,
deliver my soul!"

Gracious and righteous is the Lord, and our
God is merciful.

The Lord preserves the simple; when I was
brought low, He saved me.

Return, O my soul, to your rest; for the
Lord has dealt bountifully with you.

For He has delivered my soul from death,
my eyes from tears, my feet from
stumbling;

therefore, I desire to please the Lord in the
land of the living.

☦ ☦ ☦

PSALM 116B (115)

I believed, therefore I spoke; but I was
greatly humiliated.

I said in my anger, "Every man is a liar."

What shall I render to the Lord for all that
He has given me?

I will take up the cup of salvation and call
on the name of the Lord.

I will pay my vows to the Lord in the
presence of all His people.

Precious in the sight of the Lord is the
death of His saints.

O Lord, I am Your servant; I am Your
servant and the son of Your handmaid;
You have broken my bonds.

I will offer You the sacrifice of praise and
call upon the name of the Lord.

I will pay my vows to the Lord in the
presence of all His people,

in the courts of the house of the Lord, in
your midst, O Jerusalem! Praise the Lord!

PSALM 117 (116)

Praise the Lord, all nations! Praise Him, all
peoples!
For His mercy is confirmed on us; and the
truth of the Lord endures forever. Praise
the Lord!

PSALM 118 (117)

O give thanks to the Lord, for He is good,
for His mercy endures forever!
Let the house of Israel say, "He is good,
for His mercy endures forever!"
Let the house of Aaron say, "He is good,
for His mercy endures forever!"
Let all who fear the Lord say, "He is good,
for His mercy endures forever!"
Out of my distress I called on the Lord; the
Lord answered me and set me free.
The Lord is my helper; I will not fear what
man can do to me.
The Lord is my helper; I shall look in
triumph over my enemies.

It is better to trust in the Lord than to trust in man; it is better to hope in the Lord than to hope in princes.

All nations surrounded me; but in the name of the Lord I withstood them.

They surrounded me, surrounded me on every side; but in the name of the Lord I withstood them.

They surrounded me like bees, they blazed like a fire of thorns; but in the name of the Lord I withstood them.

I was pushed hard so that I was falling, but the Lord helped me.

The Lord is my strength and my song; He has become my salvation.

The voice of exultation and salvation is in the tents of the righteous:

"The right hand of the Lord has worked wonders! The right hand of the Lord has exalted me; the right hand of the Lord has worked wonders!"

I shall not die, but I shall live and recount the deeds of the Lord.

The Lord has chastened me sorely, but He has not given me over to death.

Open to me the gates of righteousness;
  I will enter through them and confess
  the Lord.
This is the gate of the Lord; the righteous
  shall enter through it.
I will thank You, for You have answered me
  and have become my salvation.
The stone which the builders rejected has
  become the head of the corner. This is
  the Lord's doing, and it is marvelous in
  our eyes.
This is the day which the Lord has made!
  Let us rejoice and be glad in it!
Save us now, O Lord! O Lord, lead us to
  victory!
Blessed is he that comes in the name of the
  Lord! We bless you from the house of the
  Lord! God is the Lord and has revealed
  Himself to us!
Celebrate the feast with many branches, up
  to the horns of the altar.
You are my God, and I will confess You;
  You are my God, and I will extol You.
I will praise You, for You have heard me and
  have become my salvation.

O give thanks to the Lord, for He is good,
for His mercy endures forever!

✠ ✠ ✠

PSALM 119 (118)

Blessed are those whose way is blameless,
who walk in the law of the Lord.

Blessed are those who keep His testimonies,
who seek Him with their whole heart.

For those who work wickedness have not
walked in His ways.

You have commanded Your precepts to be
kept diligently.

Oh, that my ways may be steadfast in
keeping Your statutes!

Then I shall not be put to shame, having my
eyes fixed on all Your commandments.

I will praise You with an upright heart
when I learn Your righteous ordinances.

I will observe Your statutes; O forsake me
not utterly.

How can a young man keep his way pure?
By guarding it according to Your word.

With my whole heart I seek You; let me not
wander from Your commandments.

I have hidden Your word in my heart, that I might not sin against You.

Blessed are You, O Lord! Teach me Your statutes!

With my lips I declare all the ordinances of Your mouth.

In the way of Your testimonies I delight, as much as in all riches.

I will meditate on Your precepts and fix my eyes on Your ways.

I will delight in Your statutes; I will not forget Your word.

Deal bountifully with Your servant; give me life, and I shall keep Your word.

Open my eyes, that I may behold wondrous things out of Your law.

I am only a sojourner on earth; hide not Your commandments from me.

My soul is consumed with longing for Your ordinances at all times.

You have rebuked the proud, and cursed are those who wander from Your commandments.

Take away from me their scorn and contempt, for I have kept Your testimonies.

Even though princes sit plotting against me, Your servant will meditate on Your statutes.

Your testimonies are my delight; they are my counselors.

My soul cleaves to the dust; give me life according to Your word.

When I told of my ways, You answered me; teach me Your statutes!

Make me understand the way of Your precepts, and I will meditate on Your wondrous works.

My soul melts away for sorrow; strengthen me according to Your word.

Put false ways far from me and graciously teach me Your law.

I have chosen the way of truth; I have not forgotten Your ordinances.

I cleave to Your testimonies, O Lord; let me not be put to shame.

I will run in the way of Your
commandments when You have enlarged
my heart.

Teach me, O Lord, the way of Your statutes,
and I will keep it to the end.

Give me understanding, that I may keep
Your law and observe it with my whole
heart.

Lead me in the path of Your
commandments, for I delight in it.

Incline my heart to Your testimonies and
not to gain.

Turn my eyes from looking at vanities, and
give me life in Your ways.

Establish Your promise in Your servant, that
I may fear You.

Take away the reproach which I dread; for
Your ordinances are good.

Behold, I long for Your precepts; in Your
righteousness give me life.

Let Your mercy come to me, O Lord, and
your salvation, according to Your word.

So shall I give an answer to those who taunt
me, for I trust in Your word.

And take not the word of truth utterly out
of my mouth, for my hope is in Your
ordinances.

I will keep Your law continually forever
and ever.

And I shall walk at liberty, for I have sought
Your precepts.

I also spoke of Your testimonies before
kings and was not ashamed.

For I find my delight in Your
commandments, which I love exceedingly.

I lift up my hands to Your commandments,
which I love, and I will meditate on Your
statutes.

Remember Your word to Your servant, in
which You have made me hope.

This is my comfort in my affliction, that
Your promise gives me life.

Godless men utterly derided me, but I do
not turn away from Your law.

When I think of Your ordinances from of
old, I take comfort, O Lord.

Hot indignation seizes me because of the
wicked, who forsake Your law.

Your statutes have been my songs in the
house of my exile.
I remember Your Name in the night,
O Lord, and keep Your law.
This blessing has fallen to me because I have
kept Your precepts.
You are my portion, O Lord; I promise to
keep Your words.
I entreat Your favor with all my heart;
be merciful to me according to Your
promise.
I thought of Your ways and turned my feet
to Your testimonies.
I hasten and do not delay to keep Your
commandments.
Though the cords of the wicked ensnare
me, I do not forget Your law.
At midnight I rise to praise You, because of
Your righteous ordinances.
I am a friend of all who fear You and keep
Your commandments.
The earth, O Lord, is full of Your mercy;
teach me Your statutes.
You have dealt well with Your servant,
O Lord, according to Your word.

Teach me good judgment and knowledge,
for I believe in Your commandments.

Before I was humbled I went astray, but
now I keep Your word.

You are good, O Lord; in Your goodness
teach me Your statutes.

The lies of the proud are multiplied against
me, but with my whole heart I keep Your
precepts.

Their heart is soured like milk, but I delight
in Your law.

It was good for me that You have humbled
me, that I might learn Your statutes.

The law of Your mouth is better to me than
thousands of gold and silver pieces.

☦ ☦ ☦

KATHISMA 17—STASIS II

PSALM 119/118 (CONT.)

Your hands have made and fashioned me;
give me understanding that I may learn
Your commandments.

Those who fear You shall see me and
rejoice, because I have hoped in
Your word.
I know, O Lord, that Your judgments are
right, and that in Your truth You have
afflicted me.
Let Your mercy be ready to comfort me,
according to Your promise to Your
servant.
Let Your mercy come to me that I may live,
for Your law is my delight.
Let the godless be put to shame, because
they have transgressed against me
unjustly; as for me, I will meditate on
Your precepts.
Let those who fear You turn to me, that
they may know Your testimonies.
May my heart be blameless in Your statutes,
that I may not be put to shame.
My soul languishes for Your salvation; I
hope in Your word.
My eyes fail with watching for Your
promise; I ask, when will You
comfort me?

For I have become like a wineskin in the smoke, yet I have not forgotten Your statutes.

How long must Your servant endure? When will You judge those who persecute me?

Godless men have dug pitfalls for me, men who do not conform to Your law.

All Your commandments are sure; they persecute me with falsehood; help me!

They have almost made an end of me on earth, but I have not forsaken Your precepts.

In Your mercy spare my life, that I may keep the commandments of Your mouth.

Forever, O Lord, Your word is firmly fixed in the heavens; Your truth endures to all generations.

You have established the earth, and it stands fast.

The day continues by Your ordinance, for all things are Your servants.

If Your law had not been my delight, I should have perished in my affliction.

I will never forget Your precepts; for by them You have given me life.

I am Yours; save me, for I have sought Your
  precepts.
The wicked lie in wait to destroy me, but I
  consider Your testimonies.
I have seen that all things come to an end,
  and Your commandment alone is eternal.
Oh, how I love Your law, O Lord! It is my
  meditation all day long!
Your commandment makes me wiser than
  my enemies, for it is mine forever.
I have more understanding than all my
  teachers, for Your testimonies are my
  meditation.
I understand more than my elders, for I seek
  Your commandments.
I hold back my feet from every evil way in
  order to keep Your word.
I do not turn aside from Your ordinances,
  for You have taught me.
How sweet are Your words to my taste,
  sweeter than honey to my mouth!
Through Your precepts I gain
  understanding; therefore I hate every
  false way.

Your word is a lamp to my feet and a light to
my path.

I have sworn an oath and confirmed it, to
observe Your righteous ordinances.

I am sorely afflicted; give me life, O Lord,
according to Your word!

Accept my offerings of praise, O Lord, and
teach me Your ordinances.

My soul is continually in my hands, and I
have not forgotten Your law.

The wicked have laid a snare for me, but I
do not stray from Your precepts.

Your testimonies are my heritage forever;
yes, they are the joy of my heart.

I incline my heart to perform Your statutes
forever, to the end.

I have hated transgressors, but Your law I
have loved.

You are my hiding place and my defender; I
hope in Your word.

Depart from me, you evildoers, and I will
keep the commandments of my God.

Uphold me according to Your promise, that
I may live, and let me not be put to shame
in my hope.

Help me, and I shall be saved, and I will meditate on Your statutes continually.

You spurn all who go astray from Your statutes; yes, their cunning is in vain.

I have regarded all the wicked of the earth as transgressors; therefore I love Your testimonies.

Nail my flesh with the fear of You, for I am afraid of Your judgments.

I have done what is just and right; do not leave me to my oppressors.

Uphold the welfare of Your servant; let not the godless oppress me.

My eyes fail with watching for Your salvation and for the fulfillment of Your righteous promise.

Deal with Your servant according to Your mercy, and teach me Your statutes.

I am Your servant; give me understanding, that I may know Your testimonies.

It is time for the Lord to act, for they have broken Your law.

Therefore I love Your commandments above gold, above fine gold.

Therefore, I direct my steps by all Your
    precepts; I hate every false way.

Your testimonies are wonderful; therefore
    my soul seeks them.

The unfolding of Your words gives light; it
    imparts understanding to the simple.

With open mouth I pant, because I long for
    Your commandments.

✠ ✠ ✠

KATHISMA 17—STASIS III

PSALM 119/118 (CONT.)

Look upon me and have mercy on me, as is
    Your good pleasure toward those who love
    Your name.

Order my steps in Your word, and so shall
    no wickedness have dominion over me.

Deliver me from the wrongful dealings
    of men, and so shall I keep Your
    commandments.

Shine the light of Your countenance upon
    Your servant and teach me Your statutes.

My eyes shed streams of tears, because men
do not keep Your law.

Righteous are You, O Lord, and right are
Your judgments.

You have appointed Your testimonies in
righteousness and in all truth.

My zeal consumes me, because my foes
forget Your words.

Your promise is well tried in the fire, and
Your servant loves it.

I am small and despised, yet I do not forget
Your precepts.

Your righteousness is righteous forever, and
Your word is truth.

Trouble and anguish have come upon me,
but Your commandments are my delight.

Your testimonies are righteous forever; give
me understanding that I may live.

I cry with my whole heart; hear me,
O Lord! I will keep Your statutes.

I cry to You; save me, that I may observe
Your testimonies.

I rise before dawn and cry for help; I hope
in Your words.

My eyes are awake before the morning that
I may meditate upon Your promise.

Hear my voice according to Your
lovingkindness, O Lord; in Your
judgment give me life.

They draw near who persecute me with evil
purpose; they are far from Your law.

But You are near, O Lord, and all Your
commandments are true.

Long have I known from Your testimonies
that You have founded them forever.

Look on my humiliation and deliver me, for
I do not forget Your law.

Judge my cause and deliver me; give me life
according to Your promise.

Salvation is far from the wicked, for they do
not seek Your statutes.

Great are Your tender mercies, O Lord; give
me life according to Your justice.

Many are my persecutors and my
adversaries, but I do not swerve from
Your testimonies.

I look at the faithless with disgust, because
they do not keep Your commandments.

Consider how I love Your precepts! Give me life according to Your mercy.

The sum of Your word is truth, and every one of Your righteous ordinances endures forever.

Princes persecute me without cause, but my heart stands in awe of Your words.

I rejoice at Your word like one who finds great spoil.

I hate and abhor falsehood, but I love Your law.

Seven times a day I praise You for Your righteous ordinances.

Great peace have those who love Your law; nothing can make them stumble.

I hope for Your salvation, O Lord, and I love Your commandments.

My soul keeps Your testimonies; I love them exceedingly.

I keep Your precepts and testimonies, for all my ways are before You, O Lord.

Let my cry come before You, O Lord; give me understanding according to Your word!

Let my supplication come before You;
  deliver me according to Your word.
My lips will pour forth praise, for You have
  taught me Your statutes.
My tongue will sing of Your word, for all
  Your commandments are right.
Let Your hand be near to save me, for I have
  chosen Your precepts.
I long for Your salvation, O Lord, and Your
  law is my delight.
Let my soul live, that I may praise You, and
  let Your ordinances help me.
I have gone astray like a lost sheep; seek
  Your servant, for I have not forgotten
  Your commandments.

✠ ✠ ✠

We hope you have enjoyed and benefited from this book. Your financial support makes it possible to continue our nonprofit ministry both in print and online. Because the proceeds from our book sales only partially cover the costs of operating **Ancient Faith Publishing** and **Ancient Faith Radio**, we greatly appreciate the generosity of our readers and listeners. Donations are tax deductible and can be made at **www.ancientfaith.com**.

To view our other publications,
please visit our website: **store.ancientfaith.com**

 ANCIENT FAITH RADIO

Bringing you Orthodox Christian music,
readings, prayers, teaching, and podcasts
24 hours a day since 2004 at
www.ancientfaith.com

Soul of a Leader